BEST-KEPT SECRETS OF
VENICE

Publisher and Creative Director: Nick Wells
Project Editors: Sara Robson and Cat Emslie
Art Director and Layout Design: Mike Spender
Digital Design and Production: Chris Herbert
Copy Editor: Anna Groves
Proofreader: Siobhán O'Connor
Indexer: William Jack

Special thanks to: Chelsea Edwards and Victoria Lyle

18 17

5 7 9 10 8 6

This edition first published 2009 by
FLAME TREE PUBLISHING
6 Melbray Mews
Fulham, London SW6 3NS

www.flametreepublishing.com

Flame Tree Publishing is an imprint of Flame Tree Publishing Ltd.

© 2009 Flame Tree Publishing Ltd.

ISBN 978-1-84786-647-9

Printed in China

Hugh Palmer (author and photographer) is one of the world's leading photographers of landscape, architecture and gardens.
His work has been published in many magazines and reviews, including *Harpers and Queen*, *Country Life* and *World of Interiors*.
He has also carried out a host of book commissions, including *Barcelona: City of Dreams*, published by Flame Tree, and many titles
in the *Most Beautiful Villages* series, published by Thames & Hudson. His photographs have also featured in Flame Tree's
Best-Kept Secrets of Tuscany, *The Secrets of Provence* and *The Secrets of the Greek Islands*.

BEST-KEPT SECRETS OF
VENICE

Hugh Palmer

FLAME TREE PUBLISHING

CONTENTS

INTRODUCTION

For centuries visitors have flocked to Venice, curious to see if this city of fantasy can possibly exist in the real world. It does, poised so miraculously between the sky and the water that its survival through recent centuries of decline is almost as miraculous as its previous ascent to a position of imperial might, let alone the unlikely story of its birth and growth. Growth in stature, but not in size – the city, especially the ancient, central part of it, is still on a medieval scale, its treasures packed in such concentration that the visitor may become exhausted after marvelling at so much beauty and, in the busy months of the year, by the number of people who have come to marvel at the same time.

In this case, the wisest thing to do is to use the excellent water-bus service to explore the far reaches of the lagoon. The wide open spaces and the welcome breeze, as the *vaporetto* churns across the shallow water, will refresh the spirit – but this is also a chance to see the lagoon as the first Venetians saw it. The loneliest and furthest islands are barely inhabited: Torcello, once the capital, is now home to only a few dozen people. It still has its most wonderful basilica, founded in 639, whose campanile can now be climbed. From here one can look out over the bare mud flats where the first Venetians settled – an unlikely habitat, and not one they would have chosen were they not refugees, having abandoned their houses and livelihoods on the mainland, rather than face destruction by invading barbarians. It is difficult to relate this featureless wasteland to the majestic city that rises only 13 kilometres (seven miles) to the south, but take a look at the sinuous curves of the channels cut through the mud by the tides: the Italian word for such a channel is *canale*, 'canal' in our world, a word for a dull, rectangular affair, designed by an engineer to do a job. For the Venetians, it is a form of nature, the most beautiful feature of a city famous for its beauty, that will cause every visitor to fall instantly in love, as the Grand Canal reveals the extraordinary, dreamlike procession of palaces, at once flamboyant and exquisite, that line its sensuously curvaceous length.

This marriage between man and nature was made of necessity – the sea was from the first the Venetians' only defence against the invading hordes – but the relationship continued to flourish: fishing sustained them; trading enriched them; before long their seamanship was taking them far beyond the confines of the Adriatic. Their ability in trade and their city's position as the easiest trans-shipment point from oceangoing to lagoon-going craft made their position as merchants doubly fortunate. They soon built up a powerful navy to protect their merchant fleet and, by audacious campaigning, took over islands and ports where they could establish their own network of trading posts. The administration of what became an empire required a bureaucracy as artful and intricate as Venice's own political system. The byzantine complexity of the division of power was so successful that during the many centuries of its imperial might, despite the huge potential rewards, no coup d'état succeeded in wresting power away from the council. In reality it was an oligarchy: the original merchant classes formed themselves into a nobility whose prestige and wealth were shown off in their magnificent *palazzi*. But it was the wealth and prestige of the city-state that came first, and there was a sound mercantile reason for the magnificence of its architecture and artefacts – a dazzling way to show off its power, and the confidence and solidity of its banking system. But even while visiting potentates were marvelling at the gilded excesses in the Palazzo Ducale, they never saw the secret goings-on behind the facade. A special guided tour, the 'secret intinerary', now allows visitors into the tiny plain wood-panelled office where the Chief Minister ran the whole show. This man, elected by a more than usually complex system of ballots, was paid more money than anyone else in the whole of Venice – much more than the Doge, who for all the magnificence of his trappings was appointed merely as a figurehead. The modesty of this tiny room was supposed to have reminded its incumbents that the minister's work was for the glory of the republic first, that the individual was a servant and that disloyalty would prove fatal.

Despite Venice's long reign as a global maritime power, her pre-eminence could not last for ever. Increasing competition in trade meant that the empire was losing ground, although it continued to put on a handsome display. After the ravages of fire and plague (sent as a divine punishment, according to some), the city fell into the well-chronicled excesses of debauchery, as the last descendants of the merchant families squandered their remaining fortunes in the casino, in company with the decadent aristocracy expelled from other failing empires. A new empire then emerged, a new type of ruler rose to autocratic power in Europe, and the old order was unable to resist. When Napoleon ranged his artillery against the city, the council capitulated. He bled Venice of whatever could be turned into cash to fund his continuing imperial campaigns, and added insult to injury by

It may turn out that it is this, rather than a literal flood, that will prove to be the most threatening for Venice's future. There are environmental dangers all too apparent: after the particularly disastrous *aqua alta* of 1966, it was found that previous decades of industrialization on the mainland, as well as poisoning the lagoon with effluents, had carried on such uncontrolled water extraction that the entire lagoon was literally sinking underneath the city. This compounded the devastating effects of high tides coming in from the Adriatic, whose level rose 10 centimetres (four inches) in the last century.

But it is too early to write an obituary of Venice, however elegiac: the city plays too great a part in our collective imagination to be allowed to disappear. The famous Venetian ingenuity, which first dreamt up the wooden foundations on which the city was built, is right now devising a system of tide barriers that will discourage the *acqua alta* from further threatening the ancient fabric of the city. But conserving the structure and curating the artworks for ever-increasing floods of visitors to enjoy will not

carting away to Paris the great bronze horses that had been adorning the top loggia of the Basilica San Marco since 1240, when the Venetians had looted them after the Sack of Constantinople. What potent symbols they were, of turning fortunes! Venice was robbed of her dignity; her people reduced to a state of near beggary and starvation. Napoleon later paid the final insult, giving away title to the city and her remaining territory to the Austrian Empire, as a job-lot part of a larger treaty. Despite the miserable conditions endured by the Venetians, visitors still came – some indeed attracted by the air of faded glory and gradual decay which was an inspiration to the nineteenth-century English and German Romantics. After the proud independence of Venice was symbolically ended by the construction of a causeway from the mainland in 1846, the small trickle of tourists who had arrived by water became a great flood, now arriving by train, and later by car and coach.

save the city from dying. The Venetians are leaving, discouraged by lack of opportunity and unable to afford property prices pushed up to the skies by visiting romantics, who want to own a part of the dream. If they go, their wonderful traditions will leave with them, together with the skills, learned and mastered over so many centuries, by which they have overcome, so triumphantly, the challenges of living in a city floating on the water.

Such are the true secrets of Venice, to be discovered by the fortunate visitors who can come out of season or spend some time actually living in the city. Their money will contribute to the real economy, not just to the souvenir businesses that cater to the day-trippers. Venetian life will reveal itself gradually, to anyone with a curious eye who can wonder, as they wander, at the way the Venetians have adapted to their unique situation: above all, at the joyous bustle of boats that whizz up and down the Grand Canal, piloted with such insouciant grace by their boatmen, with that seemingly inborn skill with waterborne craft that is so many centuries old. It is expressed with the minimum of flamboyance, with such dignity, far removed from the vacuous self-expression, the orgy of histrionic hooting, that is the usual leitmotif of traffic on the mainland. Merciless is the tut-tutting of the Venetian matrons, when a trainee steersman disturbs their gossip by bumping his *vaporetto* into the landing stage: it is a universal expectation that everything will be done elegantly and beautifully, organized in the intricate, idiosyncratic Venetian way. Miraculously, there are seldom collisions, despite the throng of boats of every size and shape ... sleek water taxis, delivery barges, ambulances, hearses, postal boats, police launches, the ungainly *vaporetti* and the impossibly delicate and graceful *gondole*. For all the wealth of art and architecture to be wondered at in Venice, it is the vibrant life of the city that is the greatest marvel.

CANAREGGIO

A charming idiosyncrasy of Venice's street-naming system is that the spelling on the painted signs usually follows the vagaries of the local dialect. You are as likely to come across Cannareggio as Canareggio, Canaregio or Cannaregio as you wander through this, the largest of the city's *sestieri* (districts). It is also the most recent addition to the main city of Venice.

Compared with the close-knit medieval warren of *calli* (streets) and canals that typifies neighbouring San Marco, Canareggio boasts wide, long, straight canals, often with broad *fondamente* (boardwalks) on either side. The most Venetian and least touristic quarter of the city, it faces west towards the industrial skyline of Mestre, Venice's nearest landfall, and, more attractively, northwards, where the Fondamenta Nova looks out beyond the cemetery island of San Michele, towards the distant Dolomites.

Tucked away in this almost regular grid system is a small circular island that in ancient times, before the Arsenale (shipyard) came to be, was an important iron foundry – in fact the word 'ghetto' is said to come from *gettare*, meaning to 'cast'. In the early sixteenth century, the Venetians allowed the Jewish community to settle in this cramped neighbourhood – witnessed by the unusually tall tenements that ring the central *campo*. In those days its inhabitants were literally confined to the island, with guarded gates and a patrolled moat. Now it is home to a mixed community, although still the cultural centre for Venice's Jewish population, with schools, a library and several synagogues.

FOR ALL YOUR CARNIVAL NEEDS
On the Strada Nova

On the busy Strada Nova, bustling commuters and local shoppers actually outnumber the tourists. But few corners of Venice are so off the beaten track that they do not boast several shop windows full of these decorated masks. The city's annual *carnevale* has recently been revived, and the pre-Lenten festival brings in many visitors to admire the living, walking statuary decked out in eighteenth-century costume and fabulously elaborate masks. But although local workshops still keep up the traditional craft of mask-making, the majority of carnival paraphernalia is shipped in from the Far East to satisfy the souvenir lust of the day-trippers.

PASTICCERIA
On the Strada Nova

The Strada Nova, a wide and busy street that runs most of the way between the Rialto and the railway station, was formed partly from the filling in of canals and partly from the pulling down of some of the older, less grand houses. The order to do this was given by Napoleon himself and was designed to make what was considered at the time to be a proper boulevard. Many of the shops that line it are modern, but even an up-to-date bakery will stock pastries whose appearance and unmistakably Venetian names suggest that they have been made this way since medieval times.

FROM THE STRADA NOVA
Towards the Grand Canal

The Strada Nova gives such a convincing impression of being any shopping street in any Italian city (despite its being mercifully empty of cars) that, after following its busy course a couple of hundred metres towards the railway station, it can come as a surprise to glance left and receive an unequivocal reminder that this is indeed Venice. The view that opens up along the Rio San Felice reaches to the Grand Canal itself, and on the opposite bank is a palazzo that dates back to the eleventh century, its long history lending its facade a mixture of styles. The name, Ca' Favretto, alludes to the long tenancy of an eminent local artist of the nineteenth century, Giacomo Favretto.

RIO SAN FELICE
From Sotoportego dei Preti

The addition of safety measures to prevent Venetians falling
off their bridges and into the canals is not a new idea: as well
as the many sets of iron railings, which date from the industrial
age – generally the nineteenth century, during the reign of the
orderly-minded Austrians – there are many bridges, often
the more important ones, where the brick or stone parapet
is so obviously a part of the design that it must have been
constructed at the same time. It is in the less-frequented parts of
Venice, such as over this lonely canal up near the Fondamenta
Nova, that the rarity of foot traffic has meant that the bridge
has been left in its original, parapetless state.

SANT'ALVISE
From the Ponte del Capitello

The most far-flung of Venice's churches, Sant'Alvise also boasts
the most severe of Gothic facades, undecorated except for the
ogival arches beneath the eaves and the marble portal, which
contains a statue of the Franciscan saint Louis of Toulouse, to
whom the church is dedicated. The side walls of the church were
raised in the seventeenth century, to make room for the large
frescoed ceiling that dominates the interior. It is possible to
imagine the front in its original shape and see that its plainness
would have enhanced a charming simplicity, in contrast to the
ungainly facade we see now. But the interior is far from plain
and contains two superb and dramatic paintings by Tiepolo.

BY RIO PANADA
Parrocchia Santa Maria dei Miracoli

Close by the Miracoli church, the windows of an old
merchant's house, decorated in the classic style of the
Venetian Gothic, look out over the canal. Not many houses
of this size can boast a garden, albeit one that is almost too
small to sit in, but the opening it creates between buildings
affords enough space for the sun to make an occasional
appearance. This area is at the extreme eastern end of
Canareggio: a few yards away, the busy Rio dei Mendicanti
marks the boundary with neighbouring Castello.

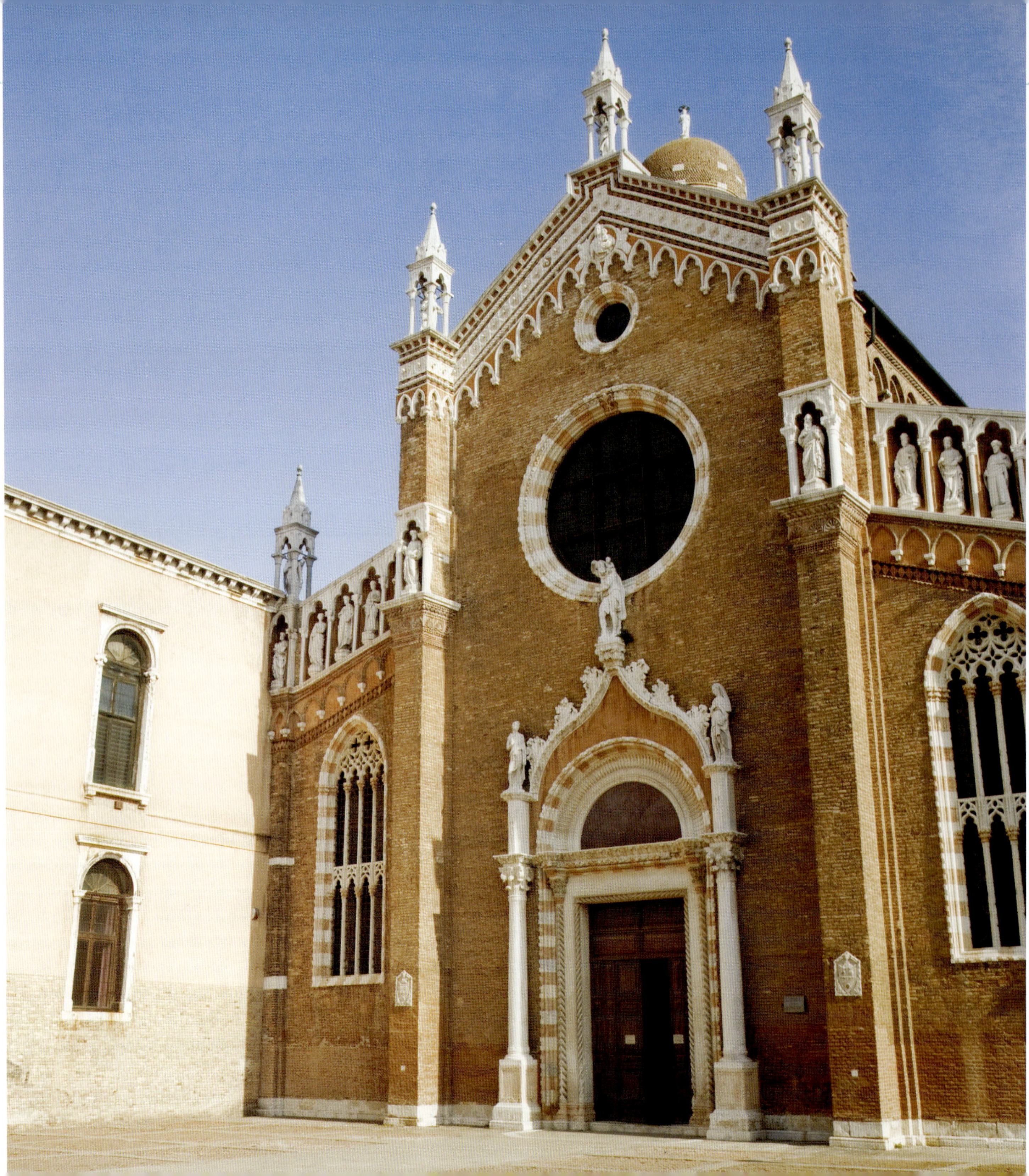

MADONNA DELL'ORTO
From the Ponte dei Mori

Among the many fine marble statues that adorn the beautiful
late Gothic facade of the Madonna dell'Orto church is the
figure of Saint Christopher, placed centrally above the porch.
Formerly, this church was dedicated to him, as the patron saint
of the boatmen who used to land here having crossed the
northern Lagoon. But after a series of miracles was connected
with a statue of the Holy Virgin that stood in a vegetable plot
(*orto*) close by, the church was rededicated. The facade was also
remodelled and took its present form, much admired, around
the year 1400.

RIO PRIULI
Parrocchia Santi Apostoli

Houses were built on many storeys from the earliest beginnings
of Venice's creation, as the mud flats that served as the first
foundations were of limited size. The high-building custom was
followed even when later housing was added, as in the case of
these houses that are facing each other across the narrow canal
of the Rio Priuli. As a result, sunshine gains access to the houses
for only a limited time each day. Despite, or perhaps because of,
this, many of the windows sport a cheerful display of flowers.

THE GRAND CANAL
From the Scalzi Bridge

Merchant houses and *palazzi* along this stretch of the Grand
Canal, many of which have been converted into hotels, enjoy a
Grand Canal frontage as well as access, on the land side, to the
Lista di Spagna. This lively street, now often lined with souvenir
vendors due to its proximity to the railway station, owes its
name to the former Spanish embassy (now the regional
government headquarters) to which it leads. The embassy almost
lost its diplomatic status in 1618, when it was discovered that
the ambassador of the time was plotting to bring in Spanish
soldiers, disguised as civilians, to lend muscle to a plot to
overthrow the Republic.

RIO TERA BARBA FRUTARIOL
Parrocchia Santi Apostoli

Considerable changes to the fabric of the city took place
during the nineteenth century, after the Republic had been
handed over by Napoleon to the Austrian emperor. The Austrians
had their own ideas about replanning Venice, and it was during
their tenure that the railway link effectively put an end to her
geographical independence. Among other attempts to bring the
city into line with its mainland counterparts was the filling in
of many of the smaller canals. The picture shows the width
of paving that now stretches out in front of houses that
formerly had only a narrow *fondamenta* running along the
edge of the canal.

RIO DEI MIRACOLI
Towards Campo Santa Maria Nova

This tranquil canal is a popular spot for beginning or ending a gondola ride. Gondoliers often moor their craft here, beside the bridge that leads over on to the Campo Santa Maria Nova. This is a quiet part of town, but one full of hidden treasures, and few visitors will fail to be delighted by the sudden sight of the exquisite marble-clad exterior of the Miracoli Church (*see* page 26). There are few ways to experience this as pleasantly as to recline against the tasselled cushions of a gondola and look upwards at the elegant panels of multicoloured marble as you silently slide by.

SANTA MARIA DEI MIRACOLI
From the Ponte dei Miracoli

This exquisite church has, thankfully, been left in its original form, although it would be difficult to conceive of any restoration scheme that could possibly improve on the design of Pietro Lombardo and his sons, who finished their work here in 1489. The cladding of richly coloured marble panels (showing resplendently after a recent cleaning) can be admired on all four sides of the church – a rare treat, as many of Venice's churches are built in close proximity, or are attached, to other buildings.

RIO DE CANZIAN
From the Calle Larga Widmann

One of the advantages of hiring a gondola in a more remote part of Venice is that sliding along the quiet backwaters will reveal tantalizing glimpses along truly hidden canals visible only from the water. On the other hand, the amazing bustle of a trip along the Grand Canal will provide its own excitements, probably of a less tranquil kind, as the gondola can seem like a frail and sinkable vessel when a huge and heavily laden delivery barge or, still more alarming, an impatient water bus is bearing down. This, however, is an ideal opportunity to observe closely the steering skills of the gondolier, as well as his unruffled composure.

CAMPO DI GHETTO NUOVO
Parrocchia Sant'Alvise

The large community of Jews, which was granted its own neighbourhood at the beginning of the sixteenth century, had to cram itself on to a very small island, and built very tall tenements as a result. Inside the confines of Ghetto Nuovo they found room for the five synagogues that still survive here – two in use and three dedicated to guided tours for those who make the pilgrimage to the world's first ghetto. The central *campo*'s spaciousness may come as a surprise, especially after entering the ghetto through one of its cramped entrances (*see* right). Many of its inhabitants left during the city's economic decline in the nineteenth century, and several of its residential blocks were pulled down after decaying beyond repair.

ENTRANCE TO THE GHETTO NUOVO
Parrocchia Sant'Alvise

The unusually tall buildings of the Ghetto Nuovo, as well as the tiny entranceway through which one has to enter, give an idea of the layout and function of this, the first ever ghetto. When the Venetian council decided to allow this small island (once the site of a foundry) to become the home of the city's scattered Jewish community, it was for sound business reasons. The Jews were able to lend money at interest, an activity traditionally denied to Christians, so their presence was encouraged, albeit strictly controlled. They were expected to pack their dwellings on to this small island and to be confined to the area, whose entrances were manned by armed sentries (paid for by the inhabitants).

RIO DE LA SENSA
Parrocchia San Marziale

This canal is one of three canals, with the Rio della Misericordia and Rio della Madonna dell'Orto running parallel to the north, that were laid out in a regular plan after an area of swampland to the north-west of the city was reclaimed during the eleventh and twelfth centuries. The celebrated churches of the area, Santa Maria dell'Orto and the tiny Sant'Alvise, would originally have been built on islands separated from the main city, but can now be approached on foot along these pleasantly wide and straight canals.

CAMPO DELL'ABBAZIA
Parrocchia San Marziale

Close to the northern edges of the *sestiere* of Canareggio, this beautiful little square owes some of its wistful air to the two ancient buildings that dominate it, both of which have been closed for many years. The church, ancient indeed, having stood here in various forms since the tenth century, was formerly attached to the Scuola of Santa Maria della Misericordia, which sits beside it. This dates back to the early fourteenth century, but was left vacant when the Scuola moved into a bigger, far uglier building that still bears the Scuola's name, although it is now used as a sports hall.

TEATRO MALIBRAN
Parrocchia San Giovanni Christostomo

Play-going and, more particularly, opera-going were central to the social life of the Venetian nobility, so it is no surprise to learn that there were four theatres, including the famous Il Fenice, still in operation when the Republic fell at the end of the eighteenth century. This one, the Teatro Malibran, fared better than most, and remained open throughout the Austrian occupation. Originally it was called the Teatro San Giovanni Christostomo, after the parish church nearby, but in the 1830s it was renamed in honour of a famous mezzo-soprano of the era, the Spanish singer Maria Malibran.

ANTICA STAMPERIA DI GIANNI BASSO
Calle del Fumo

The contents of Gianni Basso's print shop in the Calle del Fumo provide a fairly comprehensive overview of the history of printing, going back at least two hundred years. But Signor Basso would hate to see his presses and trays of type lying idle, and is not one's idea of a yawning museum curator, as he darts energetically about the narrow confines of his atelier, using his collection of antique presses (all rescued from printing shops with a lesser will to survive) to produce exquisite hand-printed stationery and books. 'Qui, Venezia!' he proclaims proudly. 'Là,' gesturing dismissively in the direction of the tourist honey pot of San Marco, 'Taiwan!'

BY THE CANAL DI CANNAREGIO
Parrocchia Santa Maria dei Penitenti

After the railway viaduct was built, the natural approach to the northern part of the Lagoon from the western end of the Grand Canal was blocked to water traffic, so the main canal of the *sestiere* is a vital cut-through to the Lagoon, and is usually busy with laden barges, as well as water buses. Just to the north, however, at the extreme north-west tip of the city, residents of the new housing blocks that have been built on reclaimed marshland can enjoy an uninterrupted view out over the Lagoon, as well as a quiet life in one of the least-visited parts of the city.

SANTA CROCE & SAN POLO

The westernmost *sestiere* of Santa Croce has suffered particular indignities in meeting the twentieth century's need for a 'modern infrastructure'. It lost several churches, including that from which it takes its name, to the construction of the Piazzale Roma, that sprawling concession to the needs of the motorist. Nevertheless, there are some charming areas to be discovered here – not least the characterful and lively *campo* (square) that surrounds its main remaining church, dedicated to Santa Maria dell'Orio.

Santa Croce is often paired with neighbouring San Polo, within whose bounds lies the first area to be identified as the commercial centre of Venice: the Rialto (from the Italian *riva alta*, meaning 'high bank'). This was the most suitable point along the course of the Grand Canal for the transfer of goods from seagoing to lagoon-crossing craft.

Close by the Rialto Bridge is the traditional market area of Venice, to which the fruit and vegetables still arrive each morning as they have always done, along the main thoroughfare of the Grand Canal. Fish and seafood are sold in a covered market hall close by. Although the pollution of the Lagoon's waters during the past century has consigned the local fishing industry to the history books, Venetians have happily lost none of their traditional ability to do wondrous things in the kitchen with the 'fruits of the sea'.

THE GRAND CANAL
Looking north from the Rialto Bridge

With the elegant campanile of the Santi Apostoli punctuating the skyline, the Grand Canal continues on its upward stretch, above the Rialto Bridge. Although it is a treat to admire the procession of elegant *palazzi* (palaces) from water level, whether from a bobbing gondola or a crowded *vaporetto*, the view from the bridge itself is always fascinating. It is an ideal opportunity to marvel at the sheer variety of the water traffic: private launches, high-speed water taxis, lumbering delivery barges, undertakers' hearses and postmen's boats – all manage to weave between each other in a spontaneous but perfect ballet.

THE RIALTO BRIDGE
By the Riva del Vin

A gondolier squeezes in among his rivals' craft moored along the Riva del Vin, strategically positioned for the horde of visitors who will head for the Riva's cafés and restaurants after they have explored the Rialto Market. The famous bridge has been a much-loved feature of the Grand Canal since it was erected at the end of the sixteenth century, after a competition was organized by the state authorities. The winning design, by the appropriately named Antonio da Ponte, managed to blend in with the wide variety of styles that line the Grand Canal here, as well as supporting two arcades of shops on its broad back – not to mention being in perfect structural condition today.

THE ERBERIA
Rialto Market

The fruit and vegetable section of the Rialto Market is positioned within easy reach of the jetties alongside the Grand Canal, allowing access for the endless succession of delivery barges that start unloading from the earliest hours of the morning. There is no nostalgia about the ancient market's popularity with the householders and restaurateurs who flock here in such numbers: the stallholders have as keen an eye for supreme quality and competitive pricing as do their customers, and few markets in Italy can surpass the range of ingredients on show. This holds even more true for the *pescaria* (fish market) further down the quay.

BY THE RIALTO BRIDGE
Alongside the Riva del Ferro

The jetties along the Grand Canal beside the Rialto Bridge attract almost as much water traffic as the Rialto Market. There is a restriction on the amount of unloading that can be done on San Marco's actual water frontage, the Molo, so the deliverer of this cargo of drinkables is looking for the nearest berthing point on the Riva del Ferro, from which the crates and barrels can be unloaded to be pushed along the narrow streets of the main shopping street, the Mercerie, on the trolley waiting on the barge's prow.

THE RIALTO BRIDGE
From the Riva del Vin

The Rialto area was also a centre for Venice's international mercantile interests – almost as long ago as the food markets began (there is evidence that the markets were well established by the eleventh century) but which has not had the same staying power. After the first bank, the Banca Giro, was opened here in the early twelfth century, dozens of others followed and, in the period of maritime exploration and the opening up of fresh trade routes, the Venetian bankers were ideally positioned to provide speculative capital for new ventures. The discovery by Vasco da Gama of the route to the Orient round the Cape of Good Hope caused the immediate collapse of many of the Venetian investors.

THE GRAND CANAL
Looking towards the Rialto Bridge

On the left of the Grand Canal, the majestic procession of *palazzi* reveals itself along San Polo's bank. Happily for the gondoliers steering their *traghetto* across to the Sant'Angelo landing stage, there is a lull in the morning rush-hour throng of water taxis and delivery barges. But it is peak time for the number of foot passengers on their daily commute, and it is easy to see why it would be impossible for a single oarsman to attempt to move this amount of human cargo across the canal quickly enough to avoid being a dangerous hazard.

BY THE RIALTO MARKET
From Campo San Giacomo di Rialto

As the Rialto was the first area to be settled in what has now become Venice, it is not surprising that its parish church, San Giacomo di Rialto, is supposed to be the oldest-established in the city, thought to date from as far back as the fifth century. Glimpsed from its little square, a waiting gondolier shows the pride of his calling, with characteristic lack of self-consciousness at being dressed in his traditional costume (albeit accessorized by dark glasses and jacket).

GIARDINI PAPADOPOLI
Parrocchia San Nicolo Tolentino

A refreshing sight for travellers newly arrived at the Piazzale Roma bus station, this rare patch of greenery occupies the site of the original Santa Croce church, of which a fragment of wall runs along the Fondamenta del Croce, on the Grand Canal side. This was once a private garden, mentioned in old guidebooks as being open by appointment. The wealthy family to whose palace the garden belonged eventually extended their generosity by bequeathing the whole to the Venetian State.

SAN GIACOMO DELL'ORIO
From the south side of the campo

Both geographically and in terms of acting as community meeting place, the Campo San Giacomo dell'Orio has become the de facto centre of what remains of Santa Croce's *sestiere*. The pretty square has a good supply of cafés and restaurants, and there is usually much boisterous activity from the younger residents. The church which the *campo* surrounds on three sides is an ancient one, and was being rebuilt as early as 1225 to allow the incorporation in the transept of a giant column of *verde antico* that was part of the booty brought back from the sack of Constantinople.

RIO DE SAN APOLLINARE
From the Sotoportego del Tamossi

If navigating these quiet canals in the heart of San Polo by water, the visitor would be well advised to ask his or her gondolier to turn left down the Rio dei Meloni. A short way down its length, the Campiello dei Meloni opens up to reveal in its corner the tiniest and most enchanting of Venice's many *pasticcerie*, or pastry shops. The Rizzardini family, whose shop first opened its doors a mere two hundred years ago, make a speciality of their *frittole*, doughnuts studded with pine nuts, raisins and candied peel, traditionally enjoyed by Venetians during the pre-Lenten excesses of *carnevale*.

THE FRARI
Gothic aedicula on the roofline

The huge size of the Frari, like that of its Dominican equivalent of Santi Giovanni e Paolo, can be a little overpowering at first sight, particularly as this church, unlike the other, is often approached from under the arches of the Calle Larga, bringing you up close to the soaring walls of mostly unadorned brick. But if you look upwards, the massive effect is relieved by the Gothic brick and marble decoration under the eaves, and the sprightly marble *aedicule* that, despite their more severe context, suggest those on the front of the Basilica San Marco.

BY THE FRARI
From the Calle Larga

A local artist has found a perfect place in the sun beneath the high brick walls of the Frari – also ideally placed to catch the eye of the art-minded visitors who flock to this great church. As mentioned, this is the companion piece to the church of Santi Giovanni e Paolo in Castello (*see* page 139): that church was built for the brothers of the Dominican order, this for the brothers of the Franciscan order, at around the same time in the mid-fifteenth century. In the sacristy, Giovanni Bellini's most celebrated altarpiece can be seen in the setting for which it was painted, and above the main altar, for those who like their Rennaissance art in its fully ripened state, Titian's flamboyant *Assumption of the Virgin*.

RIO TERA DELLE CARAMPANE
Parrocchia San Cassiano

Only 150 metres from the bustle of the Rialto, this quiet street in the *sestiere* of San Polo is home to a restaurant that lovers of traditional Venetian food have been searching out for generations – the Antiche Carampane. On the opposite side of the street, a hedge and railings block the view of a secluded private garden, the grandness of whose mansion is hinted at by the ornate but solemn caryatids who stand along the garden wall.

SCUOLA GRANDE DI SAN GIOVANNI EVANGELISTA
Above the entrance to the courtyard

The Scuola of San Giovanni Evagelista is one of the six 'grand' confraternities of Venice, which were all religiously based. This one housed a fragment of the true cross, which is still housed in the Scuola's building. *Scuole* were an important part of the Venetian social fabric, perhaps helping the stability of the oligarchy who effectively held on to absolute power over their subjects for more than 600 years. They were financed by subscription and functioned as a social service, providing health care, education and pensions to their members' families.

DIVO IOANNI APOSTOLO ET EVANGELISTAE
PROTECTORI ET SANCTISSIMAE CRVCI

PALAZZO PISANI-MORETTA
The Grand Canal

The finest, and most delicate, of the Gothic palaces of
San Polo that line the Grand Canal, the Palazzo Pisani-Moretta
nevertheless has enough boldness in the form of its symmetrical
design that it can instantly be picked out on the famous
bird's-eye view of the city made by Jacopo de' Barbari.
This remarkable work was completed in 1500, and it is worth
a visit to the Correr Museum at San Marco to admire not
only the exquisite fineness of the woodcut's detail, but also
how much of the Venice that he recorded is still unchanged
and in place today.

RIO MARIN
By the Calle San Zuane

Although the *sestiere* of Santa Croce lost its own church, as well as
several others and a few monasteries, during the development of
the Piazzale Roma on its western fringes, its heart is alive and
beating, as can be seen here along the smart rows of houses that
line the Rio San Marin. This leads up to the Grand Canal, near
the Ponte degli Scalzi, the footbridge linking Santa Croce to the
western part of Canareggio. The Piazzale Roma, without a proud
architectural tradition itself, has recently sprouted a new
footbridge of innovative and much-praised design – the first
new bridge to cross the Grand Canal for seventy years.

ON THE FONDAMENTA DEL GAFFARO
Parrocchia San Nicolo Tolentino

One of the great attractions of walking about Venice is the constant eye-catching and exotic details that adorn buildings old and new. In a sense this is part of a very ancient tradition that suffuses the whole city, radiating out from the most ancient and famous centre of San Marco. Uniquely, even in times of war, the Venetians were freed from the need to build defensively, with strong materials and massively thick walls that would withstand a siege, and they could be playful with their architecture and indulge with sensual delight in decoration that owes much to their long association with the cultures of the Orient.

RIO DELLA MADONETA
Towards the Ponte dei Cavalli

One building's depth away from this narrow canal, to the left, lies a surprisingly spacious square, the Campo San Polo, whose church gives the *sestiere* its name. Because the layout of the canals preceded any building, and the buildings were necessarily built right up to the edge of the canals to give direct access, the *calli* on their landward side will typically follow the kinks and curves of the canals. In this case, it is the *campo* whose concave eastern side echoes the curve of the Rio della Madoneta.

SAN NICOLO DA TOLENTINO
The west front

The giant neoclassical porch pasted on to the unfinished front of San Nicolo da Tolentino did not soften John Ruskin's deflating opinion of the church: 'one of the basest and coldest works of the late Rennaissance,' as he called it. Inside, the decoration of the otherwise stiffly Palladian interior is the kind of rococo riot that he would not have cared for at all. A suitable point of discussion, then, for the students of Ca'Foscari's Faculty of Architecture, who now inhabit the former convent next door.

RIO DEL PONTE DELLE BECCARIE
From the Ponte Storto

The top end of this canal, where it meets up with the Grand Canal, is a busy spot, with a queue of barges often waiting to make their way home after dropping off their loads at the *pescaria* situated by the junction. Two hundred metres away, all is calm and quiet, with the evidence of a hidden-away garden poking over an ancient wall. The lowest, canal-level floors of these buildings, built for water access and storage, are rarely inhabited, especially now that the *acqua alta* ('high water') floods them with increasing frequency.

FONDAMENTA CONTARINI
Along the Rio San Stin

Despite the intricate voting system that decided who should take up the high offices of the Venetian Republic, it should not be supposed that this was an early example of a democratic state. Although some powerful individuals shouldered their way up to power from the lower ranks of Venetian society, political control remained solidly in the hands of the merchant families who were the first to achieve wealth and status as their city grew as a centre of commerce. Morphing in successive generations into a complex, home-grown system of *soi-disant* nobility, these families gave their names to the numerous *palazzi* inhabited by their descendants. The Contarini family, for instance, after which this street is named, had no fewer than twenty-two *palazzi* bearing their name. They can truly be said to be among Venice's founding fathers, having been present at the swearing in of the first Doge in 697, and one of their own number occupying that position eight times.

RIO SAN CASSIANO
Towards Ponte delle Tette

A respectable distance away from the parish church of San Cassiano, the Ponte delle Tette ('Bridge of the Breasts') marks the centre of one of Venice's many former red-light districts, where in this case working girls several divisions below the famed courtesans of the aristocracy would sit topless at their windows. Venice was already attracting a flood of tourists during its commercial heyday in the sixteenth century, and pleasure-seekers among them could even buy a directory which gave names, addresses and details of the pick of the 11,654 state-registered, tax-paying prostitutes.

CAMPO SAN POLO
Looking towards the church

One might think that all Venice's pigeons were on permanent duty in Piazza San Marco, but a hungry flock is gathering on the Campo San Polo in the spring sunshine. The spacious square was once famous for its bull fights and jousting tournaments, and once had a *rio* (river) running along its eastern side. The white marble band interrupting the paving in the picture shows its course. It ran past the Palazzo Soranzo, which still looks out over the square. Here, a young Giacomo Casanova, playing the fiddle during a three-day ball, caught the eye of an elderly senator, who adopted him.

SAN MARCO

The smallest and most central *sestiere* of Venice is a rewarding treasure trove for the visitor who wants to escape the crowds. Even during the summer months, when it can be standing-room only in the Piazza San Marco, a short stroll can reveal the most secretive and peaceful *campiello*, from which narrow *calli* squeezing tightly between imposing *palazzi* walls may lead to a rewarding private view of the bustling Grand Canal.

Less solitary will be an exploration of the narrow Mercerie, the series of shop-lined streets that snake between the Piazza and the Rialto Bridge. The enticing window displays, often featuring the products of Venice's remaining artisans, create such a jostle of spectators outside in the narrow street that it can be a relief to venture inside, where the present-day merchants of Venice will charm you with their natural courtesy.

Right beside the Basilica is the historic centre of Venice's temporal power – the Ducal Palace. Behind its majestic facade are to be found the extraordinary displays of Venice's imperial wealth, in the vast gilded state rooms such as the *sala del maggior consiglio*, not much smaller than a football pitch and overlooked by the largest oil painting in history – Tintoretto's mighty *Paradiso*. In contrast are the less lavish rooms where the behind-the-scenes work was done, which, including a purposeful torture chamber with adjoining cells (from one of which the incorrigible Casanova famously escaped), have recently been opened to visitors.

THE CAMAPANILE OF SAN MARCO AND THE PALAZZO DUCALE
From the Giudecca Canal

Rising like a glorious confection from the water, the ancient Palace of the Doge, Venice's elected leader, is as impressive from afar as it is close up. At the time of its building, in the course of the fourteenth and fifteenth centuries, it was an audacious display of the Republic's confidence in its naval might and the security of its famous 'walls of water'. Every other head of state in Europe had to garrison him or herself inside the grim fastnesses of a siegeproof fortress. The magnificent Basilica San Marco was sited right beside the Doge's Palace – less to signify the Catholic Church's involvement with the city's politics than to show that the Doge was mighty enough to have such a church as his personal chapel.

UNDER THE LOGGIA
Palazzo Ducale

On the two sides of the Palazzo Ducale that face on to the Piazzetta San Marco and the Riva degli Schiavoni, a spacious walkway was incorporated to give the nobility and merchants a shaded area under which to walk, converse and do business. An extremely skilful restoration in the late nineteenth century enabled the pavement here to be raised by a foot to avoid its inundation by rising water levels. Even the difficult-to-please and generally anti-restoration architectural critic John Ruskin pronounced himself satisfied with the result, although it had been feared that the thirty-six supporting pillars would appear too short and squat as a result.

ACROSS THE PIAZZETTA TO THE LAGOON
St Mark's Column

From the upper loggia of the Basilica San Marco, there is a chance to look out over the Lagoon and see beyond the nearest islands of San Giorgio Maggiore, on the left, and the eastern tip of Giudecca, to the right. High above the level of the water, one of the Piazzetta's two columns bears the symbol of Saint Mark the Evangelist, the winged lion. Prior to the 'miraculous' arrival of St Mark's remains (*see* page 80), Venice's patron saint was San Teodoro, who stands with a crocodile at his feet on the neighbouring column.

THE PORTA DELLA CARTA
Entrance to the Palazzo Ducale

Seen from beneath the arches of the western loggia of the Palazzo Ducale, this scene sits above the splendid Gothic 'Paper Gate' that was the main ceremonial entrance to the *palazzo*. The centrepiece of the gate's decoration, which was completed by Giovanni and Bartolomeo Bon in 1443, it shows the incumbent Doge of the time, Francesco Foscari, kneeling before the lion of St Mark. The original sculptures were destroyed by Napoleon's troops, and the present versions are well-crafted replicas created from the numerous paintings and prints of the famous gilded and painted originals.

THE TETRARCHS
Basilica San Marco

On the corner of San Marco's Sacristry, facing the Piazzetta, this strange group of figures is one of the most familiar among the many pieces of booty to be displayed on the Basilica. Made from durable Egyptian porphyry, the statues, staring trance-like at their unfamiliar home of exile, depict the four Tetrarchs who once ruled over the Roman Empire in the era of Diocletian. The Venetians brought them home after their notorious sack of Constantinople during the Fourth Crusade, having removed them from the porch of the Philadelphion.

CEILING OF THE SCALA D'ORO
Palazzo Ducale

Clearly conceived to impress those who arrived, perhaps from faraway nations linked to Venice by trade, to do business with the Republic, the lavishly decorated main stairway leads from the first floor of the Palazzo Ducale to the second, from whose state rooms the empire was controlled. A building as unashamedly lavish as this can get away with having not one but two *piani nobili*. The design was in the hands of the architect who dominated the city through the sixteenth century, Jacopo Sansovino.

THE MOLO
From the South Loggia of the Palazzo Ducale

The front door to Venice is the Molo, the broad stone quay that served for centuries as the ceremonial landing place for visiting potentates and the city's own grand officials. Seen here from under the arches of the Palazzo Ducale's south loggia, the Bacino San Marco is filled to the brink with gondolas waiting for the day's crop of tourists to wake up and start thronging among the dozens of peanut vendors and Carnival mask-sellers who set up here.

GONDOLAS ON THE MOLO
Bacino San Marco

The distinctive prow of Venice's fabled gondola dates back to the earliest form of the craft. Made of metal (hence the prow being named *ferro*), it was designed to act as a counterweight to the gondolier standing at the stern. At various stages of the gondola's history, brass, stainless steel and aluminium have been used. The six tabs that adorn it are also commonly supposed to relate to the number of *sestieri* into which Venice has historically been divided.

LANDING AT SAN MARCO
By the Capitaneria di Porto

Seen over the south wing of the Procuratorie Nuove, the dominating campanile of Saint Mark's Basilica soars to a height of almost 100 metres (330 feet). It has stood on its commanding site since 1514 – however, not in exactly its present form, as in 1902 cracks appeared in its base and it sank gracefully to the ground, thankfully injuring no one. The unanimous decision of the council on the evening of this unwelcome event was to rebuild an exact replica – *'con'era, dov'era'* ('as it was, where it was'), in the expression that has become a favourite Venetian saying.

THE DOMES OF SAN MARCO
From Piazza San Marco

The exterior of Saint Mark's Basilica, particularly the facade which looks on to the Piazza San Marco, is a sight which almost every first-time visitor finds as breathtaking as it is familiar. As it rises up from the Piazza, its form and decoration become ever more heavenly and fantastical, to the skyline where the great domes conjure up the fabled Orient, whose treasure made the fortune of generations of Venetian merchants. Gothic enthusiast John Ruskin understandably went into ecstasies at the sight: '… the crests of the arches break into a marble foam, and toss themselves far into the blue sky in flashes and wreaths of sculptured spray…'.

MUSEO MARCIANO
Basilica San Marco

The four great bronze horses of San Marco now live inside the Basilica, their original places on the loggia overlooking the Piazza now taken by some convincing replicas. Few *objets d'art* deserve an uneventful retirement as much as these four horses, once the plunder of the Roman Emperor Constantine from an unknown ancient site in Greece. From their place on top of Trajan's Arch in Rome, they found their way to Constantinople, where they were part of the loot carted off by the Venetians after their sack of the city in 1204. Napoleon made a point of stealing them during his imperial conquest, and they were only returned to Venice in 1815.

THE TORRE DELL'OROLOGIO
Piazza San Marco

Recently emerged from its temporary shrouding during a prolonged period *in restauro*, Venice's central timepiece is once again showing off its resplendent face, as well as the mechanical excellence of its innards. The movement was commissioned by Doge Agostino Barbarigo, who desired that 'a most excellent clock' should be built on the Piazza, at the entrance to the main shopping street, the Mercerie. Envious rival powers put about the fabricated tale that the two clockmakers, father and son Giampolo and Giancarlo Rainieri, had their eyes put out after the completion of the masterpiece to prevent them repeating or surpassing their achievement elsewhere.

PORTA DI SANT'ALIPIO
Basilica San Marco

There is only one remaining original Byzantine mosaic of the four that once stood above each of the four main doorways to the Basilica San Marco. It is worth choosing this doorway because, looking up, one can see a contemporary view of how the Basilica looked in its earliest incarnation, before the Gothic additions and decorations were added to the skyline. The mosaic also shows the triumphal arrival of Saint Mark's body at its new home, having been stolen and smuggled out of Alexandria by two Venetian merchants in the year 828.

SEMPER SE

FROM THE CAMPO SAN VIO
Across the Grand Canal

CORTE CORNER
Parrocchia San Samuele

Opposite the Campo San Vio, one of the rare *campi* on the Dorsduro that can boast a view directly on to the Grand Canal, two modest *palazzi* each boast the traditional water gate that gives access to the motor boat tied up outside. The acquisition of a licence to pilot one's own craft on the waters of the Lagoon, although an insignificant investment compared with the cost of purchasing, let alone keeping up, a residence looking on to the Grand Canal, nevertheless requires some careful navigating through the intricacies of Venetian bureaucracy.

A peaceful oasis of greenery and ancient well heads, this charming courtyard lies at the end of the *calle* Corner o del Magazen, which leads nowhere else and could easily be passed by because it has the air of not leading anywhere. Such is the delight of ambling aimlessly around Venice, off the beaten track of major cultural 'must-sees'. Note the perforated marble slab, part of the ingenious design that enabled each Venetian *campo* to store its own supply of fresh rainwater in an underground cistern, essential in a city surrounded by 'water, water everywhere, and never a drop to drink'.

CAMPO MANIN
Parrocchia San Luca

This square used to be named after the church which stood nearby, the Chiesa San Paterian. After this was pulled down, the square was renamed in honour of the fiery Venetian patriot Daniele Manin, who was born in a house on the square, towards which the statue by Luigi Borro gazes intently. It was Manin who, after the Austrian occupation had lasted more than forty years, led the citizens' revolt that resulted in the capture of the Arsenale, the expulsion of the Austrian Governor and the (temporary) re-establishment of the Venetian Republic.

FROM THE SALUTE
Across the Grand Canal

The Grand Canal is rarely empty at any time of day. The myriad craft on which Venice depends for all her day-to-day needs rely on its ample size and direct access to the main trading areas. Delivery barges pass by carrying anything from casks of wine to grand pianos. Once goods get as near to their destination as the canal permits, the final negotiation of the *calli* is achieved by transferring to handcarts. Here a lightly laden local boat makes its way purposefully past some yet-to-wake-up *palazzi* near the San Marco end of the canal.

PONTE AND CALLE GIUSTINIAN
Rio di San Vidal

Close by the San Marco end of the Accademia Bridge, the small square of the Campo San Vitale heads off towards neighbouring Campo San Stefano and the main thoroughfare towards the Piazza San Marco. Running off discreetly to the left, however, is the narrow bridge and Calle Giustinian, named after the Palazzo Giustiniana-Lolin to which it leads. This is now in the hands of the Ugo and Olga Levi Foundation, which has succeeded in tracking down and returning to their home several of the original paintings by Jean Raoux that were commissioned by the Giustinian-Lolin family at the beginning of the eighteenth century.

THE SCALA DEL BOVOLO
Palazzo Contarini-Minelli del Bovolo

The full name of this fourteenth-century Gothic *palazzo*, Contarini Minelli del Bovolo, which includes the Venetian dialect word for 'snail shell', suggests that its well-known spiral staircase has always been associated with the building. In fact, this wonderful construction was added much later, around 1500, to a design by Giorgio Spavento, the architect of the church of San Salvatore nearby. The view from the top, although a mere five storeys above ground level, is nevertheless very well worth the enjoyable effort involved in discovering the *palazzo*, which is well hidden down a minuscule *calle* off the Campo Manin.

LAMPSHADES, FORTUNY STYLE
Calle delle Ostreghe

The lovable Greco sisters have been running their small
specialist shop close to the Ponte delle Ostreghe for more
years than one can tactfully inquire. Inside, their delightful
handmade lampshades are piled high, next to a selection of
traditional lamp stands. Angela Greco greets her customers,
while in a back corner, cordoned by teetering stacks of
lampshades, her sister Rita works away with glue, wire and
scissors. Now, as always, they use only the famous fabric
produced by the Fortuny factory, which happily is still in
production over on the island of Giudecca.

ANTIQUE SHOP
Salizada San Samuele

The small streets of Venice secrete many hidden treasures. Here is a tiny shop filled with carefully selected original items from the ancient *palazzi* and churches of the city – displayed to tempt the new tenant, perhaps, of one of the old houses that are increasingly ending up in the hands of well-heeled incomers. This can mean a one-off source of funds for a struggling Venetian family, but more importantly the promise of survival for a precious part of the city's architectural heritage, as ancient walls are saved from collapse and derelict interiors once more glow with life and colour.

RIO DI SAN LUCA
Ponte de la Cortesia

Close to Campo Manin, part of the main walkway leading from the Ponte dell'Accademia to the Rialto Bridge, a pair of bridges crosses the Rio di San Luca. Tucked away to the left of the picture is the rarely visited church dedicated to the parish's patron saint. The church often appears in Turner's Venetian sketchbooks, not necessarily because of its visual charm, but more likely because the English artist used to stay near San Marco, and this canal was his usual chosen route to cut through to the Grand Canal.

CAMPO SAN STEFANO
Statue of Nicolo Tommaseo

After the great Piazza San Marco, this square is the largest in the *sestiere*. Usually thronged with a mixture of hurrying Venetians and wandering visitors, it is also on the main thoroughfares between San Marco and the Ponte dell'Accademia. The imposing figure standing thoughtfully atop his plinth is one of the most popular heroes of the Risorgimento, Nicolo Tommaseo. The sculptor intended the pile of books at his feet to signify the learned basis of his political ideas. Every generation of Venetian schoolchildren, however, has grown up knowing this familiar landmark as the *Cacalibri* (the 'book-shitter').

LEGATORIA PIAZZESI
Campiello della Feltrina

Proudly boasting its historical credentials as the oldest bookbindery in Venice, the shop and atelier close to the church of Santa Maria del Giglio was first opened in 1851. Under the spirited direction of psychologist/poetess Lavinia Rizzi, great-granddaughter of one of its co-founders, it continues to produce hand-printed paper using the carved wooden *stampi* which her team of artisans painstakingly anoint with coloured inks. The atelier itself is open only by appointment, but the shop is a heavenly retreat in which to browse among the floor-to-ceiling displays of paper artifacts.

FROM THE FOOT OF THE ACCADEMIA BRIDGE
Looking across to Campo San Vitale

Immediately opposite the Ponte dell'Accademia, the silent campanile of Can Vitale stands beside its now deconsecrated church. A fine painting of the same saint by Vittore Carpaccio can be viewed inside what has now become an art gallery, although most Carpaccio enthusiasts will be hurrying by, eager to feast on the incomparable masterpieces of Saint Ursula's life story and *The Miracle of the Holy Cross at the Rialto Bridge* waiting for them over the bridge in the Accademia di Belle Arti.

FROM THE ACCADEMIA
Across the Grand Canal

Tucked away close to the San Marco side of the Accademia Bridge, the modest-looking two-storey house in the picture receives many a covetous glance from the visitors who look down on it as they cross the bridge. It has the distinction of having not only a frontage on the Grand Canal itself, but also its own private bridge giving access across the Rio di san Vidal. As if this were not enough, it boasts its own small garden – a tremendous rarity, particularly in this central part of the city.

PALAZZO FRANCHETTI
From the Ponte dell'Accademia

The flamboyant flag-adorned Palazzo Franchetti that
dominates the view from the Ponte dell'Accademia is an
example of the fashion for neogothic architecture that swept
Europe in the nineteenth century. Here in Venice, in
proximity to so many exquisite paradigms of the real thing,
its stylistic shortcomings are more apparent. The baron
Franchetti who commissioned the restoration left the palace
to his son Giorgio, who did not care to live there, instead
devoting his energies and much of his family's fortune to the
(extremely sensitive) restoration of the wonderful Ca' d'Oro.

RIO DEL CAVALLETTO
Beside the Bacino Orsoleo

Just behind the Piazza San Marco, this little canal is the
nearest that the canal system manages to get to the busy centre
of the city. Just along the canal, there is now a small canal basin,
always full of waiting gondolas, the Bacino Orseolo. Before it
was built in 1869, this must have been a congested spot indeed,
as gondolas thronged to pick up and deposit their passengers
and cargo. As always, it is a surprise as well as a relief to find
such a peaceful scene only paces away from the high-season
mayhem of the Piazza.

ATELIER ROLANDO SEGALIN
Calle dei Fuseri

This excellent repository of living artisanship is to be found in
the Calle dei Fuseri not far from Piazza San Marco. Rolando
Segalin's father founded the tiny, cramped workshop in 1932,
and it is still in operation, now under the artistic supervision of
his apprentice, Daniela Ghezzo, a young Venetian who trained at
the Accademia delle Belle Arti. Working mainly to commission,
she and her small team often create designs that challenge the
limits of the shoe-enthusiast's imagination, while still adhering
to the traditional handworking techniques of the city's artisans.

DORSODURO

The 'hard back' of this district's name refers to the relative solidity of the mud flat into which its wooden foundations were originally sunk, an inference that might be taken from the grandness of the merchants' houses and *palazzi* that have been built here. Certainly it is now the most exclusive and high-priced residential area of Venice. It is no 'Nob Hill', however, in terms of feet above sea level: in times of *acqua alta* you are just as likely to find your hotel ankle-deep in flood water here as in other more low-rent areas of the city.

To the south, the Dorsoduro is bounded by a broad *fondamenta* named the Zattere – a glorious suntrap for enjoying a midday pizza while looking out across the sparkling waters of the wide Giudecca Canal. Opposite, the large island of Giudecca is a hotchpotch of modest residential quarters, boatyards, the remnants of once-glorious gardens of the nobility on its south side and the sporadic and often abandoned factories that marked nineteenth-century Venice's attempt at industrialization.

The Dorsoduro proper is home to two of the most celebrated treasure houses of Venice: the baroque masterpiece of Santa Maria della Salute, which presides majestically over the seaward end of the Grand Canal; and the equally huge Galleria dell'Accademia. The churches and *scuole* of the city are so richly endowed with wonderful paintings that it is a shock to find so many more here – another indication of the extraordinary length, breadth and depth of the Venetian empire's artistic patronage.

RIO DI SAN TROVASO
From the Fondamenta Priuli

Tucked away behind the Palazzo Loredan, but with nevertheless an oblique outlook on to the Grand Canal, the well-lived-in look of this ancient merchant house's facade is made beautiful by the early afternoon sunlight. The smart green-and-white striped mooring poles belong to the neighbouring Hotel Accademia, popular for its offering of a small garden, from which breakfasting guests can also peek out at the toings and froings on the Grand Canal.

CHIESA DI SAN TROVASO
The south pediment

The Chiesa di San Trovaso boasts two matching facades, remodelled in the seventeenth century, which present a utilitarian albeit elegant face to the world. The two entrances, this one giving on to the spacious *campo*, the other on to the *fondamenta* running along the Rio di San Trovaso, were reputedly designed to accommodate the churchgoing needs of two fiercely rivalrous local families, the Nicolotti and the Castellani. The church's original dedication, to the saints Gervasio and Protasio, gave it an unwieldy name, before the local dialect abbreviated it with a characteristic lack of logic.

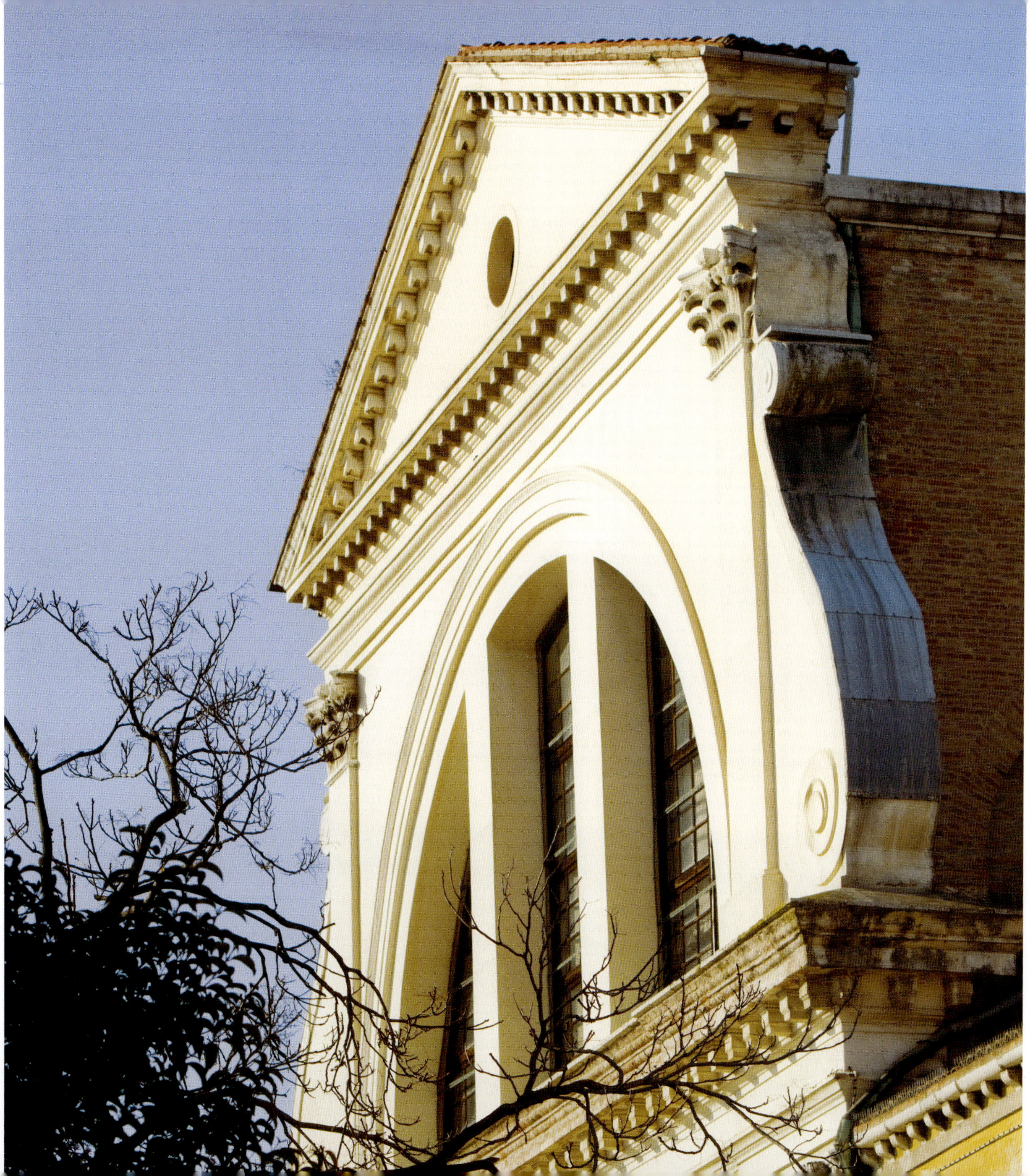

THE ZATTERE AND SAN TROVASO'S CAMPANILE
Across the Giudecca Canal

The sunlit attractions of the Dorsoduro's Zattere are apparent even at a remove across the wide Giudecca Canal. The bridge that links the Zattere al Ponte Longo to the Zattere ai Gesuati allows the Rio di San Trovaso to form a link with the Grand Canal. The two matching facades of San Trovaso's church are visible, as is its bell tower, which, in common with many of its confrères about the city, has developed a list as a result of the uncertainty of its foundations, optimistically sunk as they were in the mud floor of the Lagoon.

SQUERO SAN TROVASO
From the Fondamenta Nani

A tiny door off the Campo San Trovaso gives barely a hint of
what lies within. But the jumble of low wooden buildings
visible on the junction of the Rio di San Trovaso and the Rio
degli Ognissanti nevertheless represents a rare survival from a
hugely important Venetian activity – the building and upkeep
of gondolas. The craftsmen of the *squero* still make each gondola
entirely by hand, using eight different types of wood. Available
carpentry skills and materials also explain the wooden buildings
around the boatyard – a rarity in Venice ever since the
devastating fires of the early twelfth century.

ALONG THE ZATTERE
Zattere al Ponte Longo

One can imagine the outcry, among romantically minded early
tourists at any rate, when Venice made the decision to introduce
electric street lighting to bring the city into line with its
mainland counterparts. Doubtless the Venetians who had to live
there through the winter months were glad of the change.
Happily the designs of the period have endured as well as the
materials used and the lamp standards have become a familiar
and much-loved part of the visual landscape.

ZATTERE AL PONTE LONGO
Towards San Basilio

Wandering among the labyrinth of *calli* that form the older parts of Venice is a delightful way to discover the city, but it must be said that one does not have to be claustrophobic to feel, after a while, in need of some wide open spaces. The broad promenade of the Zattere on Dorsoduro will provide instant relief, particularly during a postprandial stroll to shake down one of the pizzas that are a speciality of its restaurants.

TRAGHETTO AT THE CA'REZZONICO
The Grand Canal

Gondolas that have reached pensionable age may end up
in fairly dignified semi-retirement (although with their
distinctive prow and stern decorations removed), in service as
traghetti, the ferry boats that cross the Grand Canal at strategic
points along its length. Moving as they do across the main
stream of river traffic, they need to be able to manoeuvre out of
the way quite nimbly, so are rowed by two boatmen instead of
the usual one at the stern. Standing room only for passengers
(tasselled cushions are not included in the one-euro fare) means
that good balance is required to remain upright.

SANTA MARIA DELLA SALUTE
From the Accademia Bridge

Dominating the narrow tip of land that forms the end of the
Dorsoduro, the massive baroque masterpiece of the Salute
church has been a sober and beautiful counterpoint to the
excitements of San Marco ever since it was commissioned in
thanksgiving for the end of Venice's second great plague in
1630. The winning architect of the competition held to decide
its designer, Baldassare Longhena, described his creation (in his
winning submission) as, 'a virgin work … curious, worthy and
beautiful, made in the form of a round monument that has
never been seen, nor ever before invented, neither altogether,
nor in part, in other churches in this most serene city'.

PALAZZO DARIO
From the Grand Canal

The pretty elevation we see from the Grand Canal was refaced with coloured marble at great expense and remodelled according to the newly arrived Rennaissance style when Giovanni Dario, secretary to the Venetian Senate, purchased it in 1486. The Barbaro family took it over after Dario's death, it having passed to his daughter, who married Vincenzo Barbaro. This family kept it in its possession until the nineteenth century.

PALAZZO DARIO
From the Campiello Barbaro

The attractive little square on to which the back rooms of the Palazzo Dario look out still bears the name of the Barbaro family. Intriguingly, the rear elevation has little in common architecturally with the Renaissance front; its windows and decorative features remain true to the building's original Gothic style. The much-loved palace could tell stories from its more recent history: it was owned by legendary pop impresario Kit Lambert during the heady Sixties and Seventies.

RIO DEGLI OGNISSANTI
Looking towards the Ognissanti

The narrow doorway seen behind the figures across Campo San Trovaso is the understated pedestrian entrance to that dramatic survival from a bygone age, the Squero San Trovaso (*see* page 106). Behind is the larger and later of the two churches that have stood on the Zattere and held the somewhat misleading name of Gesuati. The first church, properly named Santa Maria della Visitazione, was indeed built by the order of the Jesuits, but, after the dissolution of their order in 1668, the Dominicans took over their land and built this replacement, finished in 1743.

BY THE PONTE DELL'ACCADEMIA
The Grand Canal

A gondolier demonstrates the skill resulting from a long training and an obvious inherited flair – long family lineages of famous gondoliers are not uncommon in Venice. Here, he steers his delicate craft into the narrow entrance of Rio di San Vio, where he will tie up by the Ponte del Forner to await a fresh cargo of visitors. There is generally a steady stream of potential customers making their way to the Salute church from the Ponte dell'Accademia, seen here in the background.

SANTA MARIA DEL CARMINE
Parrocchia Santa Margherita

The Gothic church with the tall seventeenth-century campanile dates from the thirteenth to the fourteenth century. Its founders, the Carmelites, were originally hermits who lived in the desert around Mount Carmel – hence their name – and sculptures of the prophets Elisha and Elijah – thought to be the founders of the order – can be picked out along the church's roofline. Forced out of the Holy Land, they formed a mendicant order which was allowed to establish itself in Venice, as were the Dominicans and the Franciscans. Besides their church and monastery, they built a sizable *scuola*, which adjoins the church, to house their lay confraternity.

PALAZZO BALBI
The Grand Canal

This confident-looking Renaissance palace has the distinction of occupying a perfect position at the point where the Grand Canal takes a sharp bend on its way from San Marco towards the Rialto. This earned it the questionable privilege of hosting the newly arrived ruler Napoleon, who watched the annual regatta from the balcony. Less fortunate was the original Balbi who built it: he tried to hurry up the construction work by living on a boat tied up alongside, but caught a chill and died before he could achieve his aim.

ON FONDAMENTA NANI
Parrocchia San Trovaso

Venice's population has now become the most aged in all of Europe, a problem now almost as well known as the city's struggle to save its architectural fabric from sinking beneath the waves. Many would envy this little girl, making her way home from school along the Fondamenta Nani, her enchanted childhood, surrounded by beauty and insulated from many of the more disagreeable aspects of modern life. Whether she and her own children will be able to live and work in the city of their birth is another question, one which will affect the future of Venice as surely as the success or otherwise of the new flood barriers planned at the entrances to the Lagoon.

RIO DI SAN BARNABA
Ponte ai Pugni

Not far from the Campo Santa Margherita, and thus assured of a plentiful flow of passers-by, is moored one of the floating market stalls that one comes across at intervals, tied up along the canals of Venice. The ancient name of the bridge behind, Ponte ai Pugni, commemorates the traditional site where rival clans would settle their differences with their fists. The bridge still bears marble footprints to mark out the starting positions; the ending position of at least one of the combatants may be guessed – the iron railings are a more recent addition.

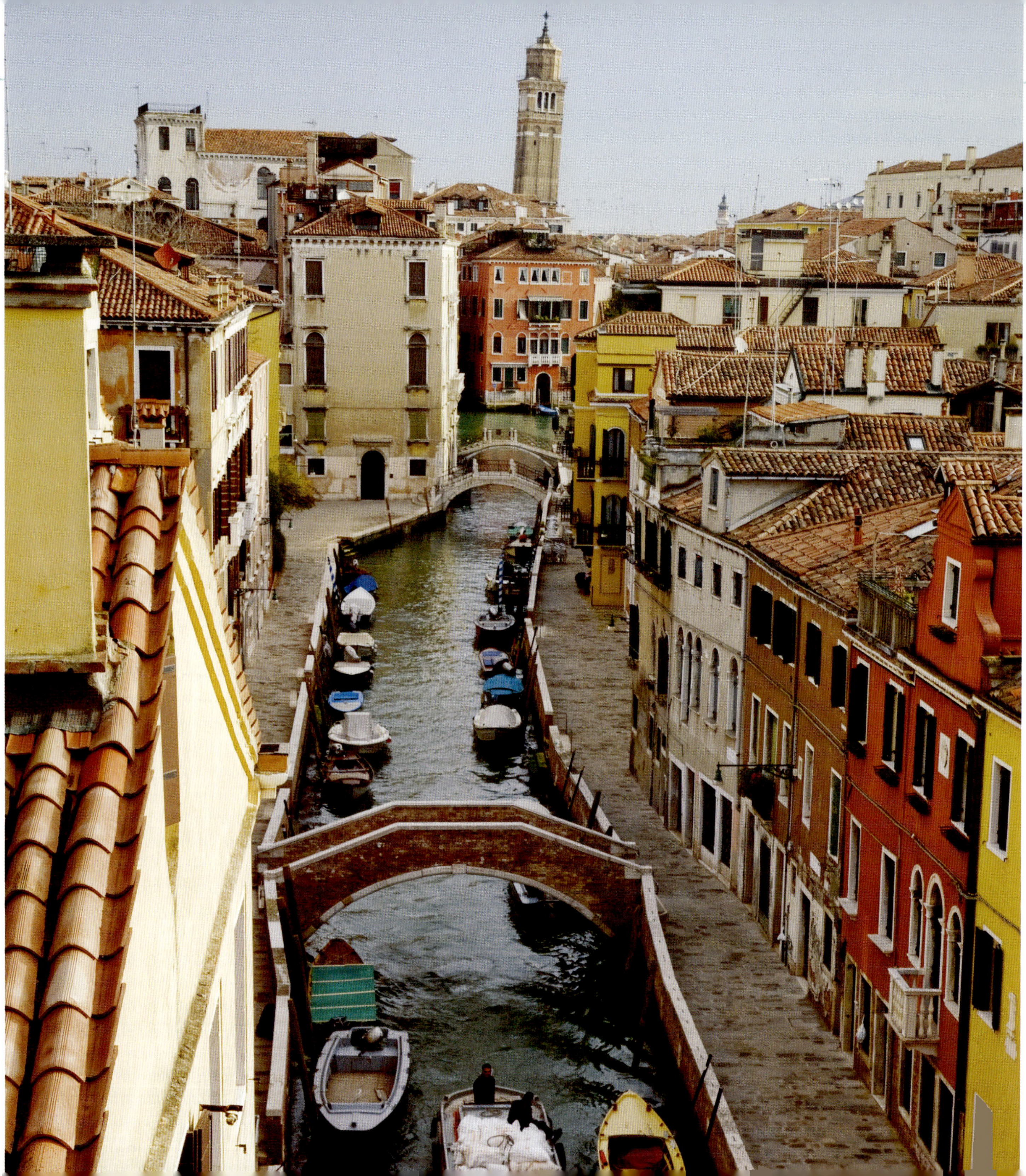

RIO DI SAN VIO
Parrocchia Sant'Agnese

The city of Venice is made up of hundreds of islands, divided by canals, some of which mark the original creeks that separated two adjacent islets. Some, like this one, were cut across the land to form a convenient waterway. The Rio di San Vio connects the Grand Canal with the Giudecca Canal and is rarely to be seen without a delivery barge making its way between the moored boats. Later in the day, a sociable pair of gondoliers will generally moor up on the left, just before the far bridge (*see* page 127).

IL REDENTORE
Across the Giudecca Canal

Palladio's most beautiful Venetian church was commissioned in thanksgiving after the dreadful plague that started in 1575 and claimed the lives of almost 50,000 of the city's inhabitants. Each July, on the anniversary of the city's deliverance, a festival is held for which a bridge of boats is assembled across the 300-metre (900-feet)-wide Giudecca Canal. People cross in their thousands to visit the church, and in the evening the canal is filled with gaily illuminated boats, which provide the best view of a spectacular fireworks display.

PALAZZO GIUSTINIANI AND CA'FOSCARI
The Grand Canal

Two of the most splendid masterpieces of the late Venetian Gothic stand proudly beside one another on the Dorsoduro side of the Grand Canal. The Giustiniani came from a family that liked to claim that its roots went back to the rulers of the Byzantine empire. They were definitely a force to be reckoned with from the earliest years of the Venetian Republic. There are no fewer than twelve Giustinian *palazzi* in Venice, not including the one next door, which was sold to the Foscari family 600 years ago. This has now become a central part of the city's famous university.

ZATTERE AI SALONI
From the Giudecca Canal

The ancient name 'Zattere' comes from the local word for rafts, and a possible connection has been suggested from the fact that salt from the Lagoon made its final journey on rafts, which tied up here while the precious cargo was transferred to its storage place in the giant Maggazini del Sale, or Saloni, which dominates this part of the *sestiere* and is just to the left of this picture. Today, part of it has been turned into art studios, while its original connection with the water makes it an ideal boathouse for one of the city's thriving rowing clubs.

GONDOLIERS AT YOUR SERVICE
Piscina Forner

Two gondoliers take their ease and swap gossip as they wait for fares beside their craft, which they have docked at the Grand Canal end of the Rio di San Vio (*see* page 122). The original cost, not to speak of the upkeep, of these traditionally built boats represents a very substantial outlay, and the fee charged for a even a short ride can be off-putting, especially as every gondolier, in true Venetian style, is as expert in matters of commerce as he is deft with his oar, making any amateur efforts to negotiate the price downwards a waste of time. They are likely to be amiable, however, and most of them, if treated with respect, will display a graceful courtesy rarely to be found in the real world of the mainland.

CAMPO SANTA MARGHERITA
From the southern end of the square

The liveliest square in the Dorsoduro, Campo Santa Margherita lies away from the grandeur of the Accademia and the Salute, close to the *sestiere*'s border with neighbouring San Polo. As a result, locals hugely outnumber visitors and, after the end of the school day, the large *campo* resounds with the cheerful yells of liberated pupils. It is also a place for the local elders to congregate, gossip and survey the activities of the younger citizenry. The cut-off stump of campanile belongs to the church of Santa Margherita, now a well-patronized local arts centre.

RIO DI SANT'EUFEMIA
Island of Giudecca

The westernmost church of Giudecca is also its oldest, dating back to the ninth century. Along its quiet canal a curious archway, relic of some former noble property, interrupts the *fondamenta*. Much of this part of the island used to be the orchards, vineyards and pleasure gardens of Venice's noble families, before the land was sold and developed for housing. Apart from the grounds of the famous Cipriani Hotel at the extreme eastern tip of the island, there is only one other surviving garden, sadly fallen into disuse, which can be tantalizingly glimpsed at the end of the Rio di Sant'Eufemia.

THE LAGOON AND ISOLA SAN CLEMENTE

Looking south from the Giudecca

The rather unloved southern fringes of the Giudecca have recently benefited from the island's new popularity with rich incomers, some of whom have colonized the luxuriously converted former factories that until now have been lying idle and empty. A new boatyard and marina, the Venice Plaza, have started to do good business next to the locals' rowing club, open to the southern part of the Lagoon. The small island in the distance is that of San Clemente, which was the home of a succession of religious orders over the past centuries, before being used for a hospital, which has now been replaced by a luxury hotel, complete with golf course.

THE ZITELLE
Across the Giudecca Canal

Named for the original inhabitants of the benevolent hostel
that was built around the church, the Zitelle ('Old Maids') was
designed by Andrea Palladio and completed after his death. It
marks the mid point of the succession of Palladian frontages
that start with the Church of the Redentore (*see* pages 123 and
134) and finish triumphantly with San Giorgio Maggiore,
which sits on its own island opposite San Marco. The Zitelle
has more modest pretensions than the other two, but fits in
harmoniously with its fellows.

LA CASA DEI TRE OCCHI
Island of Giudecca

A few doors down from the church of the Zitelle and sharing a
prominent position overlooking the Giudecca Canal is this
playful pastiche of the Venetian Gothic, with a touch of Art
Nouveau to reflect the era of its construction in 1910. It was
the creation and the studio workplace of the successful painter,
photographer, architect and illustrator Mario de Maria, who
died in 1924. Its large windows, designed to maximize the
internal light of the studio, quickly gained the house its local
nickname: the House of the Three Eyes.

RIO DI SAN VIO
The Giudecca Canal

The Rio di San Vio cuts all the way across the *sestiere* of the Dorsoduro, from the Grand Canal. Here, where it meets the Canale della Giudecca, a wide footbridge connects the promenades of the Zattere ai Gesuati with the Zattere agli Incurabili. A wide expanse of water separates the fashionable Dorsoduro from the island of Giudecca, which boasts more modest housing, but is punctuated along its length by a majestic progression of Antonio Palladio's magnificent churches. Here visible is the Church of the Redentore, built in thanksgiving after the plague of 1575.

GIUDECCA CANAL
Looking west

Across the wide expanse of the Giudecca Canal, the broad promenade of the Zattere faces the Giudecca along almost all its considerable length. The noble facades of Antonio Palladio's churches, the Zitelle and the Redentore, punctuate of the view magnificently, the more eye-catching as they rise massively from the modest housing of the island. A note of bathos awaits at the extreme end of the island in the huge hulking shape of a long-disused spaghetti factory, the Molino Stucky, now much elevated from its ignominious past in its current role as a luxury hotel.

CASTELLO

Although Venice was famously protected by 'walls of water' (*see* page 67), the first Venetian settlers built a fort for good measure – the *castello* from which this easternmost *sestiere* takes its name.

The fort no longer exists, but was sited in one of the most obscure quarters of present-day Venice, Isola di San Pietro, where a longish walk, or a circular route on a water bus, will enable the curious visitor to discover a large church on the site of the original cathedral of Venice. Such was the Republic's desire to separate temporal and spiritual power that it was not until its empire had largely vanished that the seat of Venice's patriarch was moved (by Napoleon) from here to the famous Basilica next to the Palazzo Ducale.

Close by is the wondrous Arsenale, the naval depot and boatyard that built, armed and supplied the mighty Venetian fleet. In its heyday, the world's first production line could build a galley from the keel up to seagoing fitness in a single day. Stern notices, declaring an off-limits *zona militare*, keep the Arsenale strictly away from public view, a sensitivity reminiscent of the way in which the famously secretive Republic forbade its craftsmen on pain of death from divulging the secrets of their skills to outsiders. Now there is nothing to be kept from prying eyes but the melancholy sight of the vast, deserted docks and empty workshops, where once a thousand craftsmen plied their world-famed trade.

SCUOLA GRANDE DI SAN MARCO
From the Rio dei Mendicanti

The *scuola* dedicated to the patron saint of Venice was bound to be among the six major guilds entitled to the '*grande*' in their name. Its headquarters was destroyed by fire in 1485, and a subscription enabled its rebuilding during the following twenty years by the architects Pietro Lombardo, who created the lower storeys, and Mauro Codussi, who was responsible for the upper part of the facade, whose decorative cresting arches hiding the true roofline behind are reminiscent of the Basilica itself. The *scuola* was turned by the Austrians into a military hospital, and it now houses the main civil hospital for the city.

SANTI GIOVANNI E PAOLO
From the Rio dei Mendicanti

The side aisle, dome and belfry of the Dominicans' great church are visible in this view from the far side of the neighbouring *campo*. The land for the church was donated by the Doge of the time, and to return the compliment many Doges have their tombs inside its huge interior. The equestrian bronze that stands in the square was a memorial to Bartolomeo Colleoni, commander of Venice's land forces at a time when several successful campaigns had greatly increased the Venetians' territory in the Veneto. He willed a large sum of money to ensure a monument 'in front of San Marco', but was not in a position to object when the council placed it in front of the *scuola*, rather than the basilica, of that name.

THE ARSENALE
From the Rio del'Arsenale

Both the main water entrance to the mighty Arsenale and its ceremonial land entrance immediately to the left leave no doubt that they give access (or would do, were the site not still designated an off-limits *zona militare*) to an area of great importance. On this site, which was expanded in later years to a massive 32 hectares (80 acres), the highly trained and efficiently organized *arsenalati* could produce more than 20 war galleys in a single month. A very early version of a production line also ensured that each vessel would be identical, much simplifying the handling, as well as the equipping and servicing, of the fleet.

FONDAMENTA AND RIO DE LA TANA
Off the Via Garibaldi

Either side of this long, straight canal, reached by going under an archway almost hidden between two shops on the busy Via Garibaldi, are reminders of the days when the Arsenale was at full stretch, building and equipping the ships that earned Venice its imperial dominance of world trade. On the right, the massive walls protect the Tana, or rope factory, fully 300 metres (1,000 feet) long to optimize production on a grand scale. On the left is perhaps the first example of a public housing project, built here in the Middle Ages to house the workers of the Arsenale.

CAMPIELLO DEL PIOVAN
Parrocchia San Giovanni Battista in Bragora

It is rare to find a Venetian square with not one but two well heads, still more unusual when that square bears the diminutive title of *campiello*. The occurrence of a well head, generally sited in the middle of a *campo*, indicates that the *campo* was constructed around its own built-in freshwater supply. Rainwater falling on the *campo* would drain off through perforated marble slabs, be filtered through a layer of sand, to end up cleansed and *potabile* in a cistern underneath the well head. The well head was protected from contamination by sea water by a funnel-shaped lining of clay. Strict by-laws prevented the contamination of the drinking water by using a well without permission or letting animals foul the *campo*.

SANTA MARIA FORMOSA
Chapel of the Scuola dei Bombardieri

Legend has it that this church was built on the spot where a vision of the Holy Virgin in the form of a buxom woman (*formosa*) appeared to St Magnus – it is a matter of fact that this was Venice's first church dedicated to Santa Maria. The Pope was often critical of the Venetians' tendency towards sensuality rather than piety, but it is not recorded what the papal view was of the unmistakably buxom Santa Barbara that Palma Vecchio painted for the Bombadieri, to whose *scuola* the small chapel off the south transept belonged.

GIARDINI PUBBLICI
Off Via Garibaldi

Napoleon's viceroy, Eugène de Beauharnais, laid out these gardens, often referred to as the Giardini Napoleonici, clearing away the residential quarter of the city's eastern tip, together with two monasteries and four churches. It is difficult to judge whether the descendants of those displaced Venetians value the green space so bequeathed to them: it may be that Venetians are more acclimatized to their traditional visual diet of stone and water, as the park has an undervalued look about it much of the time. Every other year, however, its stock rises when half of it becomes one of the settings for the prestigious contemporary art festival the Venice Biennale.

RIO DEI SCUDI
Parrocchia Sant'Antonino

Heartening evidence of apartments lived in by real Venetian families is visible along the canals of eastern Castello. Apartments in upper storeys have an airier drying place to hand – their washing lines can cross the canal without inconveniencing the water craft that buzz regularly along the most out-of-the-way canals. A simple pulley system allows for the retrieval of the laundry, carefully and one by one, after the drying cycle is complete. Neighbours opposite, living in such intimate proximity, would be unlikely to refuse to lend a hand if the system got into a tangle.

SANTA MARIA DEI DERELETTI
Salizzada San Zanipolo

Only paces away from the main hospital of Venice, which is reached from the Campo di Zanipolo, this church was attached to one of the minor *ospedali* that were founded to care for the homeless poor, orphaned and elderly. Behind it is still a retirement home, and it has retained its local name of Ospedaletto. The facade that rears up above the narrow street is certainly dramatic, its muscular style of sculptural decoration eliciting particularly sharp criticism from John Ruskin, never a great fan of the late Renaissance, who described it as the 'most monstrous' church in Venice.

VIA GARIBALDI
The widest street in Venice

The Via Garibaldi owes its width to the canal that used to run along its centre, filled in by orders of the Napoleonic government. The extra width was considered necessary to give easier access to the new Public Gardens (also introduced by Napoleon, *see* page 145). The term 'Napoleon' needs qualifying in this context. After invading Venice and removing as much of the saleable booty as he needed to fund his military campaigns, the emperor himself swept off in search of new lands to liberate. He left behind his less ruthless stepson Eugène de Beauharnais as viceroy, albeit with the imperial mandate to change things as he saw fit, including the name of this street, which, to celebrate its filling in, became the via Eugenia.

RIO DEL RIMEDIO
Towards the Calle Querini

This colourful group of houses, following the angular course
of the Rio del Rimedio, lies at the back of the Palazzo
Querini-Stampalia, whose owners, the noble Castello family
of the Querini, could trace their residence in the *parrocchia*
of Santa Maria Formosa back as far as the thirteenth century.
They donated this palace to the city in 1869, together with a
collection of period artefacts and some lively genre paintings
that now form an interesting display of how life was lived by
Venice's aristocracy in the eighteenth century.

SCUOLA DI SAN GIORGIO
DEGLI SCHIAVONI
The chapel

This *scuola*, although not *grande*, was started by the community
of Dalmatian merchants who had always been closely involved
in Venetian trade. It found its home in the former hospital of
Saint Catherine, and its members commissioned the Venetian
artist Vittore Carpaccio to produce the famous series of
paintings showing Saint George, Saint Jerome and Saint
Augustine. They were intended to decorate this upstairs room,
but have now been permanently installed downstairs for visitors
to marvel at, while upstairs in this richly decorated chapel the
remaining members of the confraternity still meet and worship.

RIO DI SANT'ANNA
From the Via Garibaldi

Via Garibaldi is the main street of the eastern section of the
Castello *sestiere*: its width as well as the paving marking the
original position of a canal identifies it as one of Venice's *rii
tera*, or filled-in canals. It was the Rio di Sant'Anna that used
to run the length of the street – now it is just a cut-off stub
running in from the Canale san Pietro. An enterprising
floating vegetable stall has tied up as close as it can to the
shopping street, not quite in the way of the main crowds, but
at least not having ground rents to pay nor the bother of
unloading and trolleying its cargo of fresh produce.

SAN PIETRO DI CASTELLO
The cloister

Located on its own island at the extreme eastern end of the
city (discounting the landfill extension of Santa Elena), the
church of San Pietro was Venice's cathedral until 1807. The
cynical explanation for its out-of-the-way position is that the
Basilica San Marco, obviously the premier church of Venice,
was nominally the private chapel of the Doge, so it was a
hearty snub for the Pope to have this modest church as the
centre for his operations. Modest though it may have been in
its historical role, it has a noble facade, to plans by Palladio, and
a pretty (and almost always deserted) sixteenth-century cloister.

A NEIGHBOURHOOD GOOD TURN
Fondamenta de la Tana

Particularly in the more old-fashioned neighbourhoods of
Venice, of which eastern Castello is certainly typical, the
increasing average age of the local inhabitants is everywhere
apparent. Few apartment houses are equipped with any access
more easy to negotiate than the original and often poorly kept
staircases, and this can present a problem for the older residents
who are less nimble on their feet. Some can rely on the
kindness of neighbours, who can call round with shopping,
smaller items of which can be handily received without anyone
having to use the stairs.

RIO DI SANTA MARINA
From Ponte Bressana

Even when cast iron became the engineering material
of choice during the nineteenth century, there was never a
move to modernize Venice's bridges with the latest technology
on offer. It is likely, then, that this all-metal bridge spanning
the Rio di Santa Marina is a replacement for a stone original
that collapsed during the cast-iron vogue. One of the two
rii that join the Rio di Santa Marina beyond the bridge is the
Rio della Tetta, named for the Fondamenta Tetta that crosses
it, which appropriately joins up with the Calle de Santa
Maria Formosa.

CAMPO SAN FRANCESCO
Towards Campo della Chiesa

The strollers crossing the Ponte San Francesco are approaching
one of Andrea Palladio's lesser-known churches, tucked away in
a quiet part of the *sestiere*. Before they can look across the wide
square to see the church's south side, they must pass under a
raised gallery constructed in the mid-nineteenth century to
link the Convento delle Pizzochere to the Palazzo Nunciato,
which housed the Papal Legate. Both buildings were later
taken over by the military, but the Legate's historical presence
is commemorated by the playful name of a nearby lane:
Salizzada delle Gate – 'Alley of the Cats'.

PAOLO BRANDOLISIO, REMERO
Succursale Giuseppe Carli

Paolo Brandolisio is a young master of the arcane craft of
fashioning the *forcole* (literally 'pitchforks') that act as the
fulcrum against which a gondolier pushes his oar. Not only is
the *forcola* made to fit the stature and particular requirements
of the individual gondolier, but also each one is a piece of
sculpture with its individual aesthetic character. He learned
his craft from the maestro Giuseppe Carli, whose workshop
he now runs with the help of his own apprentice. Oars are
also made to measure for each gondolier and, to make his
expertise the more precious, Paolo's skills are also in demand
by the keen sports-rowing fraternity in Venice.

SAN ZACCARIA
The west front

This striking facade straddles two ages of architectural taste, as it was started by Antonio Gambella as a strictly Gothic structure and progressed as such until his death in 1481. The architect who took over was Mauro Codussi, responsible for the Scuola Grande di San Marco (*see* page 139) and more open to the Renaissance ideas that were gaining ground in the rest of Italy. The convent next door to the church acquired a dubious reputation in later centuries, which was to do with the habit of noble families of putting all their available dowry funds towards the match of only their eldest daughters. This led to a stream of well-heeled and aristocratic younger sisters joining this most fashionable of convents, and a lax regime allowed them to indulge in the many forms of licentiousness available during the decadent years of the Republic.

CALESELA DE L'OCHIO GROSSO
Parochia San Martino

The painted street signs of Venice follow their own charming logic: they universally prefer the spelling forms of the local dialect, often recording the variations thereof by spelling the same word in different ways on each sign, and sometimes they come up with an unexpected coinage to suit a particular need. What diminutive form of the standard word for street – *calle* – could be more elegant than *calesela*? This tiny alley, the 'Big Eye' of whose title remains a mystery, certainly deserves a diminutive noun to itself: arguably the narrowest in Venice, it measures just 53 centimetres (21 inches) across.

THE LAGOON

An exploration of the greater Lagoon around Venice, made effortless by the city's incomparable water-bus service, is an enjoyable way to get a sense of how its earliest human settlers constructed the archetypes of the modern city. The first inhabited islands still display the simple pretensions of the fishing communities who lived on them, long before the unlikely confluence of mercantile success and maritime exploration caused the present city to rise skywards like some unlikely proto-Manhattan.

Leaving behind the cemetery island of San Michele and disgorging most of its passengers at Murano, home of the glass-blowers, the water bus eventually makes its way to the farthest and oldest-inhabited island in the Lagoon: solitary Torcello. This was the first capital of the Lagoon and used to support a population many hundred times its present modest year-round total of a couple of dozen. Its historical importance is indicated by the majestic cathedral of Santa Maria Assunta, from the top of whose campanile the lonely wastes of the surrounding mud flats can be pondered. Nearby, many times more populous and lively, is the charming community of Burano, with its gaily painted fishermen's houses and inescapable vendors of local lacework. Lido, the long island that protects the Lagoon from the Adriatic, despite its small-town charms and its beaches, should be visited with caution – anyone who has achieved that precious Venetian dream-state may not wish to risk seeing anything as real-world as a motorcar.

SAN GIORGIO MAGGIORE
From the Bacino San Marco

The noblest of the islands that count themselves as independent from the main city of Venice, San Giorgio is nevertheless closely connected with it, and not only by reason of its proximity. When Antonio Palladio was asked by the Dominican order, which had used the island for its monastery since 982, to build a new church, he was able to give free rein to his vision of a classical temple façade that could suit the church behind, as well as make a bold visual statement that suited the position. Generations of visitors admiring the view from San Marco have certainly marvelled at the way that every change of light seems to catch and transfigure the bold design.

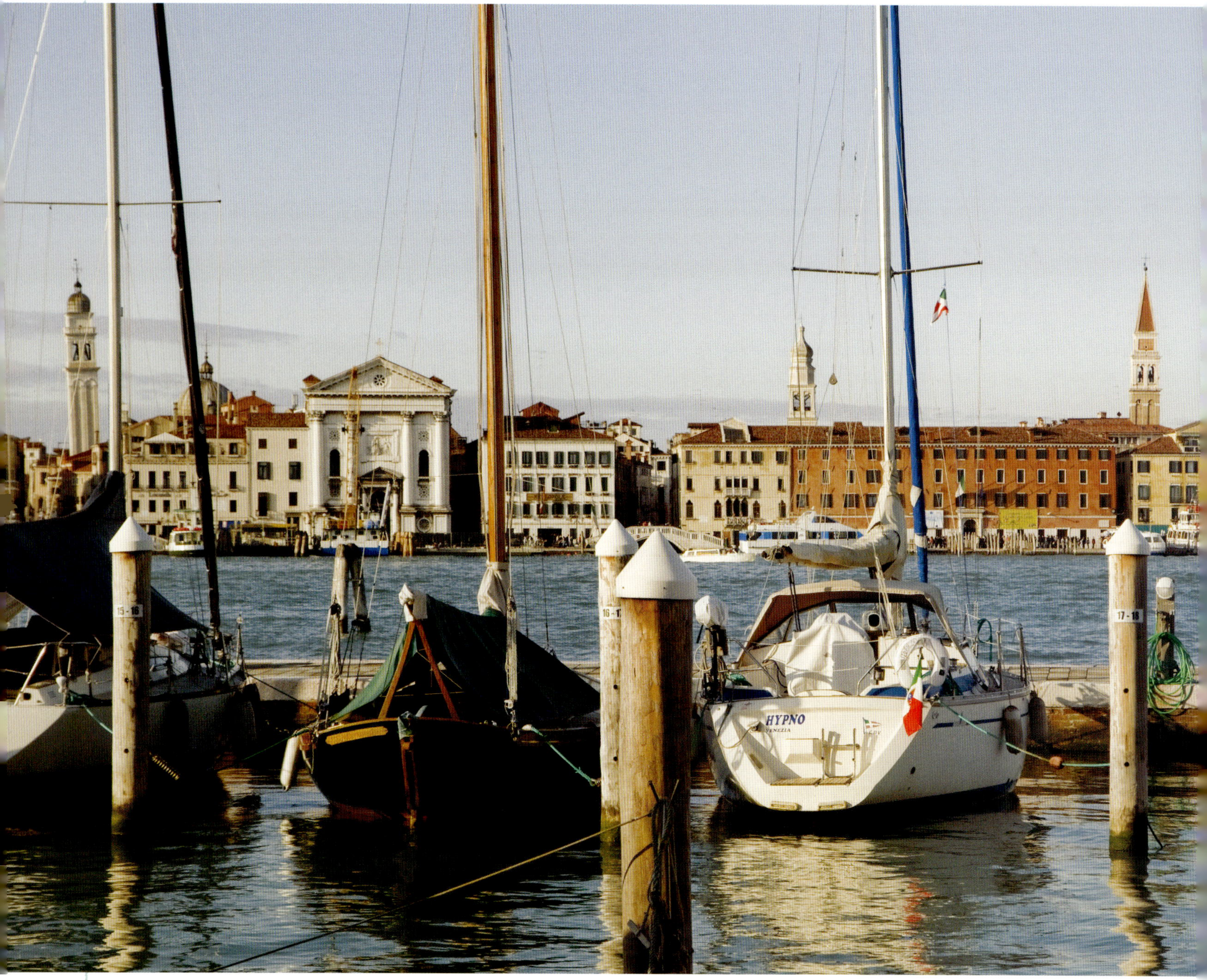
HYPNO
VENEZIA
15 - 16
17 - 18

BACINO SAN MARCO
From the Marina of San Giorgio Maggiore

If the island and church of San Giorgio are eye-catching from San Marco, imagine the sensation of waking up on your luxury yacht and looking out to see the Riva degli Schiavoni bathed in the morning light. Understandably, the marina is home to Venice's most prestigious yacht club, the Campagnia della Vela. The island of San Giorgio has further nautical ties: the Italian industrialist Vittorio Cini has established a foundation on the island that has restored many of the dilapidated buildings of the monastery, as well as setting up a naval college.

DESERTED ISLAND
The North Lagoon

Of the dozens of islands and islets that are scattered over the 500 square kilometres (190 square miles) of the Venetian Lagoon, only thirty or so are inhabited, although many show signs of having been used in the past. This tiny speck of land, close by the water-bus route into the North Lagoon, was considered dry and solid enough for a small factory to be erected, now being slowly reclaimed by the ivy and the weather. As the entire Lagoon is a protected natural site, the population of wild species is showing a healthy increase as the number of humans has declined.

THE ISLAND OF THE DEAD
Isola San Michele

Venice's traditional burial site presents an elegant, cypress-punctuated profile as viewed from the Fondamenta Nova at the northern edge of the city. From here it is possible to take a water bus to the islands of the North Lagoon, with San Michele usually the first stop. By the *vaporetto* stop, florists' stalls cater to the families who visit their departed on a Sunday after church. Until the Napoleonic reforms decreed that all burial should take place outside the city, remains were buried by the parish church of the deceased, an arrangement much preferred by the Venetians.

SAN MICHELE CHURCH
Isola San Michele

The island of San Michele has been Venice's 'Island of the Dead' only since the early nineteenth century. The architect who was to become a leading exponent of the Renaissance style in Venice, Mauro Codussi, built his first church here in 1469, when the island was used by a monastery. The church presents its smartest frontage, in Istrian white marble, to neighbouring Murano, but from the cemetery Venice's first true Renaissance church is equally innovative, an imaginative rethinking of the traditional three-lobed Gothic church common to the area.

THE CLOISTERS
Isola San Michele

The arrangement of the cemetery on San Michele (which also takes up the neighbouring island of San Christoforo della Pace – the two islands were later joined together) is based on the layout of the monastery that occupied the site from the thirteenth century. The cloister has been preserved, and is a tranquil place for a meditative stroll, although a misleading introduction to the modern reality of Venetian burial, which allows for considerably less space and privacy (*see* page 172).

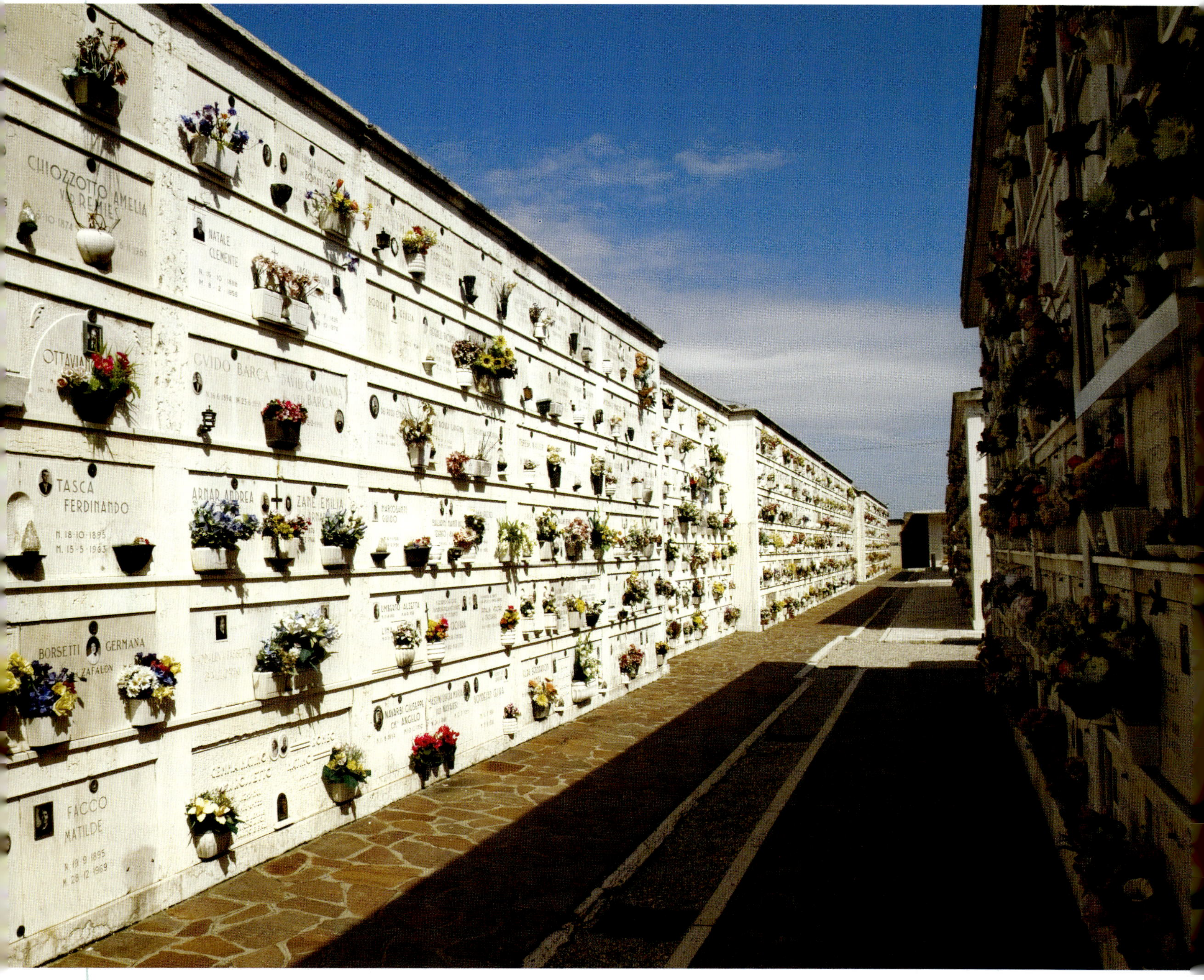
CHIOZZOTTO AMELIA
NATALE
CLEMENTE
GVIDO BARCA
TASCA
FERDINANDO
N. 18-10-1895
M. 15-5-1963
BORSETTI GERMANA
ZAFALON
FACCO
MATILDE
N. 19-9-1895
M. 28-12-1969

THE BURIAL PLOTS
Isola San Michele

The Venetians have solved the space problem concerning burying their dead in the same way as they have approached the long-standing problem of how to cram the living on to an island with a limited amount of space: by building high, limiting space per person and charging high rents. There is also a limited lease on the accommodation: after ten years, unless extra payment is made, the remains are transferred to an anonymous ossuary on a farther part of the island, to make room for a new tenant. The introduction of non-perishable floral tributes lends a strange air of macabre gaiety to the scene.

CANALE PONTE LONGO, MURANO
From the Fondamenta Andrea Navagero

Under the pennant of Venice's winged lion of San Marco, the main waterway of Murano opens up between the two islets of which the island consists. The Venetian glass furnaces were moved here in 1291 to reduce the risk of fire destroying the city, as well as to reduce the risk of the arcane (at that time) secrets of glass-blowing being sold to, or stolen by, a rival state. The glass-blowers and their families were moved here, too, housed and generally treated well – glassware was a prestigious as well as profitable export for centuries until the Venetian monopoly dried up.

CANALE SAN DONATO, MURANO
From the Ponte Cavalieri

Before the glass-blowers and their furnaces were transferred
over from the city, Murano prospered in an unusually
independent way, surviving on its fishing, the production of
salt and the charges raised in the port it operated on nearby
Sant'Erasmo. It was even allowed to mint its own coins, a rare
privilege. Even after the export of glass (mirrors and
spectacles, as well as the famous coloured beads) brought
wealth to the island, it retained enough of its rural character,
with pastures, orchards and vegetable gardens, for Venetian
nobility to build their summer homes here.

CAMPANILE OF THE BASILICA OF SANTA MARIA AND SAN DONATO, MURANO

From the Ponte Cavalieri

Around the ancient campanile of Murano's main church used to stand the medieval Palazzo del Comune, the seat of the island's partly autonomous administration, which was demolished in 1815. In its place is a war memorial designed by the Muranese sculptor Napoleone Martinuzzi. The practice of separating campanile and basilica was a rarity for Venice, perhaps because of the constant preoccupation with limited available space, the exception being the famous example in Piazza San Marco, which certainly saved one of the best-loved churches in the world from a horrible fate when the campanile collapsed in 1902.

HOW DO THEY DO THAT? COLOURED BIRDS IN GLASS, MURANO

Fondamenta Daniele Manin

When contemplating Murano glass, a balance has to be struck between admiration for the difficulties overcome in its undoubtedly ingenious production and a hesitation about whether the resulting *objets d'art* would survive the journey home – both their distinctive aesthetics and its fragile structure. As that wise Englishman Samuel Johnson famously remarked when told that a piece of violin music that he had obviously not enjoyed was very difficult: 'I would that it were impossible.'

IN THE BASILICA OF SANTA MARIA AND SAN DONATO, MURANO

By the west door

In the lofty interior of Murano's Basilica, lighting is provided, appropriately enough, by some fine chandeliers from the golden age of the island's glass production. An impression of even greater antiquity is given by the rest of the interior, particularly the floor, whose swirling mosaics are made even more dynamic by the undulations of the floor. The remarkable patterns, full of movement, colour and detail, were completed in 1141, as stated in a roundel near the centre of the nave – not much later than San Marco.

BASILICA OF SANTA MARIA AND SAN DONATO, MURANO

Exterior, the apse

One advantage that Murano's Basilica has over its more famous counterpart in San Marco is that its position means one can walk around three sides of it, admiring at close hand the delight in decoration that typifies so many of the early churches of Venice. Here, a beautiful and intricate design in brick enlivens the apse at the east end: the hexagonal form has sham arcades running around it, with nîches and double marble columns. A sensitive recent restoration has given the whole of the exterior much more of a cohesive effect than was allowed by its former, somewhat dilapidated state.

CORTE COMARE, BURANO
By the Fondamenta Cavanella

The modest pretensions of the neat fishermen's houses on the island of Burano have been enhanced, aesthetically at least, by the local tradition for painting them in gay colours. The population who inhabits them is, alas, no longer able to make its living by harvesting the fruits of the sea. The industrialization on the mainland at Mestre and Marghera has caused enough chemicals to be poured into the Lagoon to have irrevocably upset its fragile ecosystem. The skills of cooking seafood, however, have not been lost, and a good lunch awaits at one of the many *trattorie*.

CALLE TIBALDON, BURANO
From the Fondamenta Pizzo

The fashion for uninhibited colour choice in the painting of their often dilapidated houses has given the Buranese an extra attraction with which to lure visitors to their small island, particularly the artists who have been setting up their easels here for many generations. Now that the houses have been put into good repair, they have lost some of their picturesque charm. Added to which their owners have celebrated the increase in their standard of living by giving a fresh coat of paint to the outside, unfortunately with up-to-date paints whose high-tech dyes must present a challenge to the artist of today.

BY VIA DELLA VIGNA, BURANO
The island's eastern side

The island of Burano does not take long to explore, as it measures less than a kilometre end to end. Some of the more out-of-the-way lanes have older houses that have not been restored so aggressively. Here, the attractive palette of Burano can be better appreciated. A regular water-bus service linking the island to Venice, as well as the mainland, has made this an attractive place for families to settle, with its close community and lack of the less attractive features of modern life. The only economic activity directly linked to the island is the dwindling lace industry, although great quantities of lacework in all its forms are still on offer at the many tourist shops.

STRADA DEL CIMITERO, MAZZORBO
From the Burano-bound water bus

Burano's neighbour Mazzorbo, to which it is connected by a footbridge, used to be celebrated for its orchards and vineyards, and was once a popular resort for the Venetian nobility, who built many summer residences on the island. There were once a dozen churches here, although only one, Santa Caterina, survives to serve the dwindling population. A recent boost to the island's fortunes – although its fertile ground still produces fruit and vegetables – has been the excellent new communal housing project, designed by Giancarlo de Carlo in the late 1970s.

THE PIAZZA, TORCELLO
Museo dell'Estuario

Piazza may seem a grand term to describe this grassy square, but it was once the centre of the capital island of the whole Lagoon. The first settlers fleeing the Roman settlement of Altinum on the mainland chose this island to be their new home. Even when the new colony that was to become Venice was set up on the Rialto, Torcello long remained the more important trading power in the Lagoon, boasting, it was said, more than twenty thousand inhabitants. The Palazzo dell'Consiglio, which also looks more modest in scale than its title suggests, holds a collection of artefacts recovered from the island.

ON THE PIAZZA, TORCELLO
Beside the Palazzo dell'Archivio

The two former *palazzi* that were the main administrative buildings of Torcello and whose official status doubtless saved them from the stone-raiding depredations of other islanders are home to a mixed assemblage of architectural curiosities dredged up and otherwise uncovered from this remote part of the Lagoon. The ancient history of the island's settlement is reflected in the great antiquity of the exhibits, including those that have overflowed from their small *palazzi* and are displayed outside in the Piazza. Of less antiquity, despite its fanciful title, is 'Attila's Throne' in front of the Palazzo dell'Consiglio (*see page 185*).

BASILICA SANTA MARIA ASSUNTA, TORCELLO
The Chapel of the Holy Sacrament

The brilliant decoration inside the ancient Basilica of Torcello is breathtaking, despite its enormous antiquity. Here, in the chapel of the Holy Sacrament, a timeless figure of Christ enthroned blesses his flock. All the mosaic work in the Basilica, including the moving depiction of Madonna and Child on the half-dome of the apse, and the *Sturm und Drang* of the scenes of the Last Judgement portrayed on the west wall, are much increased in their beauty and impact by the decision of restorers to remove the plaster from the rest of the interior and leave the brickwork exposed, to give an idea of the plain original design.

MICHEL

ON THE PIAZZA, TORCELLO
Beside the Palazzo dell'Consiglio

This house, noble in its proportions although diminutive in size, is one of the handful to survive from Torcello's gracious past – discounting the farmhouses that are dotted over the now mainly agricultural island and the extremely gracious hotel that the Cipriani business has opened here. It suggests that it might have been one of many townhouses that were built by the locally successful merchants who were the forerunners of the princes of global trade whose *palazzi* eventually lined the Grand Canal of Venice. After Torcello's canals silted up, reducing its trading capacity, and the population was driven out by the malarial marshes, most of the houses were pulled down for building materials for the more fortunate new city.

FROM THE CAMPANILE OF SANTA MARIA ASSUNTA, TORCELLO
Looking northwards

John Ruskin was fond of visiting the lonely island of Torcello, partly for the grassy orchards where he enjoyed family picnics, partly for the sublime interior of the ancient Basilica and partly for the opportunity to muse upon the unprepossessing marshland on which the first Venetians, desperate to escape barbarian invasions, attempted to establish a safe place to live. Now that the campanile has once more been made safe, we can follow Ruskin to the top and look out over the 'waste of wild sea moor' that so inspired him.

INDEX